HOW TO KEEP YOUR INNER MESS FROM TRASHING YOUR OUTER WORLD

Bill Giovannetti

MONARCH
BOOKS

Oxford, UK & Grand Rapids, Michigan, USA

Published in association with the Books & Such Literary Agency, Janet Kobobel Grant, 52 Mission Circle, Suite 122, PMB 170, Santa Rosa, CA 95409-5370, www.booksandsuch.biz.

First published in the UK in 2008 by Monarch Books
(a publishing imprint of Lion Hudson plc),
Wilkinson House, Jordan Hill Road, Oxford OX2 8DR.
Tel: +44 (0)1865 302750 Fax: +44 (0)1865 302757
Email: monarch@lionhudson.com
www.lionhudson.com

ISBN: 978-1-85424-878-7 (UK)
ISBN: 978-0-8254-6285-6 (USA)

Distributed by:
UK: Marston Book Services Ltd, PO Box 269, Abingdon, Oxon OX14 4YN;
USA: Kregel Publications, PO Box 2607, Grand Rapids, Michigan 49501

This book has been printed on paper and board independently certified as having come from sustainable forests.

British Library Cataloguing Data
A catalogue record for this book is available from the British Library.

Printed and bound in Wales by Creative Print & Design.

To the love of my life, Margi,
and to my gifts of grace, Josie and J.D.
Every day with you reminds me how blessed I am

Contents

Disclaimer

The characters and stories in this book are composites of true people, places, and events. Names, descriptions and details have been changed to protect the anonymity of the individuals involved.

Acknowledgements

I owe a special thanks to Dave Meurer, for clearing my path into the world of writing. Thank you, Janet Kobobel Grant, for your expertise and encouragement as a literary agent. I am grateful to Dave Talbot and the team at the Mount Hermon Christian Writers' Conference, for imparting skills and catalyzing relationships that broaden the reach of the gospel through writing. Thanks go out to Tony Collins and the staff at Monarch Books and Lion Hudson for embracing this project and working so hard to make it a blessing to as many as possible.

Heartfelt thanks to many friends at Windy City Community Church – you were the first to encounter the Inner Mess with me – and to all the churches that were part of my life: Neighborhood Church, Grace Pointe Church, the North Side Gospel Center, and Grace Gospel Church. Thank you, Dave Meurer, Bob and Denise Giovannetti, Sol Cranfill, Joseph Lukowski, and Rob and Adaline Coleman for your excellent critiques. A special word of appreciation goes to Jim Dethmer and Bob Sloan for introducing many of these principles to me.

To my family – Mom, Dad, Gina, Bob and Denise – thank you for your unfailing encouragement.

A big hug and thanks to my awesome kids, Josie and J.D., for putting up with a laptop on Daddy's lap for way more hours than you should have. Let's go do something fun now. And to my most important reader, my precious wife, Margi, thank you for believing in me and for loving me, Inner Mess and all. To God be the glory.

Foreword

None of us lives without difficulty. Even for dedicated Christians, the journey can seem confusing and arduous. The Bible promises supernatural power to live above sin and circumstances, yet for many, practical holy living seems elusive at best. We struggle to unload the heavy baggage we've collected throughout our lives. We long to walk free and unencumbered in Christ, yet victory seems beyond our grasp.

The book you are holding offers tremendous hope. Bill Giovannetti approaches an old problem in a fresh way. He shines new light on God's method of cleaning up our Inner Mess – what the Bible calls, 'the flesh'. He outlines real-world wisdom for maturing in the Christ-life. In this book, you'll rediscover practical sanctification and learn how to experience authentic life in Christ, day by day.

In a writing style that is whimsical, attention-grabbing, very personal, and yet hard hitting, Bill challenges readers to honestly evaluate their Inner Mess and acknowledge how it trashes their outer world. Even more, he offers biblical solutions to invite Christ's cleansing power into your everyday life.

Bill's message is timely in light of the confusion that surrounds the topic of practical holy living. He exposes the unsavory characteristics of the inner life and then, through excellent biblical teaching, brings the reader to understand that 'Christ in you, the hope of glory' is the key to normal and fruitful Christian living. He does all of this without beating you up or putting you down.

Combining both captivating story and practical theological discourse, Bill offers an easy-to-read, engaging story that maps the road to victory. Each chapter concludes with a series of well-crafted questions that will guide you to deal with your Inner Mess, and move you forward in sanctification.

Paul states that the goal of his ministry is to bring everyone to maturity in Christ (Colossians 1:28). Without an understanding and appropriation of sanctified living, your maturity will be stymied. This book offers great hope to you – and to any Christ-follower – as you earnestly seek to be loosed from the self-life and set free to live the Christ-life.

Today's church desperately needs this message of grace-oriented holiness. The time is now. Turn the page and discover how to keep your Inner Mess from trashing your outer world.

Dr Gary Benedict, President
The Christian and Missionary Alliance, USA
Colorado Springs, CO

Part One

Meet Your Inner Mess

Anybody reared on *Sesame Street* remembers Oscar the Grouch. How can you not love a furry green monster that lives in a garbage can and breaks into a chorus of 'I Love Trash' at the drop of a hat? He would be the perfect mascot for this book, and, I suggest, for our lives. Every one of us has an Oscar within, eager to muck up our world. That's what this book is all about.

In Part One, I'll introduce you to your Inner Mess – that grouchy part of you that blurts out idiocies you regret later. You may be surprised, and even a bit depressed, to discover the mountains of trash piled in your soul. Don't despair, however. In Part Two we'll explore the formidable resources that God has provided to stop your Inner Mess from trashing your outer world.

Each chapter ends with a section called 'Taking Out the Trash', which contains questions for personal reflection and group discussion. You'll profit most from this book if you use these.

You are invited to visit the Inner Mess online community at www.innermess.com for more resources.

Happy dumpster diving!

Chapter 1
Your Inner Mess

*'No man knows how bad he is till he has tried very hard
to be good.'*

C.S. Lewis, 1952[1]

The pierced, tattooed and heavily muscled man scowled at
the bus driver and boarded without paying the fare. Scott
Thompson tried – unsuccessfully – to pretend he hadn't
noticed. But his guts tightened into a massive knot that would
take hours to untie. *Not again! What is that gang-banger doing out
of jail?*

Scott clamped his hands on the steering wheel, white
knuckles betraying the raw fear that coursed through his veins.
Did he dare pull out of the station with that felon on board?
Should he make up an excuse and order everyone off? His
mind raced through the options – all of them bad.

Scott glanced in the rearview mirror, swallowing hard as
he saw the young thug take the seat next to the elderly man in
row eight. The bus was only a quarter full. There was no good
reason for him to pick that seat. Another storm was brewing,
and Scott was being sucked into it. Again.

A primal fear climbed from his heart to his throat and
squeezed him hard...

* * *

The Bus

Let's take a break from Scott's drama and step into yours. Picture your inner life – your soul or personality – as a collection of passengers on a bus. They're not all happy. Some resent having to ride a bus in the first place. Others worry about where the bus is headed. Many of the passengers don't like each other. Sometimes it's a tense, stress-filled bus. When the bus riders in your soul aren't happy, you aren't happy. Neither are the people close to you. That's where this book comes in. I wrote it to help you stop your Inner Mess from trashing your outer world.

Many Christians sport bracelets engraved with the letters 'W.W.J.D.', posing the question, 'What Would Jesus Do?' The bracelet reminds its wearers to be like Jesus.

I hereby officially confess that, after decades of Christianity and ministry, I have tried my best to be like Jesus and have failed miserably again and again. I have often felt stuck in God's remedial program for spiritual underachievers.

I began asking why. Why does the W.W.J.D. lifestyle seem so out of reach, even for a dedicated, veteran Christian like me? The answer took me on a journey into God's Word and my own soul. What I found in God's word was liberating. What I found in my own soul was disturbing – until I started applying God's word to it; then it became liberating.

I once saw a bumper sticker that read, 'The voices inside my head are telling you to shut up.' It made me laugh. I do have voices inside my head. Not in a psychotic, get-help-now kind of way, but in a 'there's-a-lot-of-conflict-inside-me' way. What's going on inside of me isn't always pretty. It can be bedlam.

Don't look so smug. There's a little chaos inside you too, or you wouldn't have picked up a book about 'inner mess'.

Why are we such mixed bags of good and bad? Why won't all the parts of me go along with the W.W.J.D. program?

Because some of the riders on my bus are dedicated

to doing what Jesus wouldn't do. And until God transforms them, I'll never get out of his remedial class.

This book is dedicated to bringing all the parts of our personalities into harmony under Jesus Christ's leadership. Think of it as a stress-reduction program for the riders on your bus.

I've learned these truths the hard way: through dumb choices, trial and error, honest friendships, Scripture and prayer. I am confident in them, not because I have my act together – which I don't (though I would like to con you into thinking I do) – but because they arise from the Creator of the human heart. And because so many who have implemented them can tell you they work. In addition, through these principles, I'm experiencing liberty and transformation such as I've never known before.

I'm discovering how to convince my inner bus riders to relax and enjoy the ride. These discoveries are revolutionizing my life. I'm confident they will revolutionize yours too. Give it a shot. It's the only way to get out of the remedial program. In addition, it's the only way you can shepherd all the parts of you to really do what Jesus would do.

But I'm getting ahead of myself.

Meet Your Passengers
Let's back up and think more about ourselves as a collection of characters riding a bus.

The reputable characters sit toward the front: Courage, Wisdom, Generosity, Humor, Success, Patience. Each one eagerly waits to hop into the driver's seat. These characters are good for your image. You actually want them to take turns at driving.

But a host of unsavory characters have boarded the bus too. You work hard to keep them in the back seats. When these characters pop up, you cringe. Some are nasty, like your Inner Pervert, Braggart, Liar, and Bum. Some are geeky, like your Inner Nerd, Victim, Brat, and TV Evangelist. A few are snooty, like your Inner Critic, Judge, and Church Lady. A few may be dangerous, like your Inner Thug, Seductress, or Felon. No matter how hard you fight them, these malefactors clamor to jump into the driver's seat.

I'll call these characters collectively your 'Inner Mess'.

Lurking beneath your cool, calm exterior is a virtual mob scene. Just admit it: you have a creepy dark side that would give Stephen King the willies. Even if you're a Christ-follower. Even if you're a W.W.J.D. bracelet-wearer. Even if you're a pastor. You have a pierced, tattooed, heavily muscled felon just waiting to commandeer your bus.

And holding him in check wears you out.

Welcome to the world of the Inner Mess.

Your Inner Mess has a pesky habit of popping out when you least expect it, usually when it can do maximum damage to your image. And usually when you're under stress.

Such as the stress of rush-hour traffic, when I blurted out a word I don't normally blurt out.

Chicago has one of the most congested interstate interchanges in the U.S. It's nicknamed after a famous serial killer: the Hillside Strangler. The Hillside part of the name comes from the nearby suburb of Hillside. I've been told that the Strangler part comes from seven lanes of traffic merging into three. My theory is that it comes from what it makes you want to do to the drivers around you.

I was driving with two of my best friends (church friends), crawling through the Hillside Strangler. It was rush hour and we were late. I was tense, so I shifted into 'urban commando driving mode': find the lane that's moving, make rapid lane changes, beat the next guy, and don't, under any circumstances, let anybody in front of you. In Christian love.

Without signaling, a little silver sports car cut in front of me from my left and abruptly stopped. I slammed on the brakes. I also did what any God-fearing follower of Jesus would do: I leaned on the horn for a very long time.

But that wasn't all.

At the same instant, my Inner Jerk commandeered my vocal apparatus and shouted at the top of our lungs his opinion of the other driver. I did not plan this. It just happened. In a split second. Without thinking, I blurted out what I consider to be one of the top five swear words in the English tongue. My swearing was unthinking. Reflexive. Instinctive.

Swearing is not something I normally do. Especially with friends on board.

My friends gasped. Then they burst into laughter. I immediately turned red and started sweating. I was less embarrassed over my swearing than I was over getting caught. I had temporarily failed to contain the rowdy characters at the back of my bus.

'You're overreacting,' you might say. 'Swearing is no big deal'.

It was to me. Here's why: not only did I attend the same church as my friends; I was the pastor of that church. This made my slip of the tongue extra funny to them. And extra embarrassing to me. Because I'm a pastor, people expect me to keep a tight rein on the back of the bus. I am a professional at it, for crying out loud. The Hillside Strangler caused a momentary lapse of containment.

The Inner Mess's ability to pop out at the worst moments makes life nerve-wracking. What if my friends see my dark side? What would people think of me if they knew I thought – or felt or believed or did – that? It's easy to live in perpetual edit mode, always stressing over what other people think. Instead of finding the life God wants me to have, my primary mission becomes covering up the life I actually do have.

What Evil Lurks Within?

The Bible calls this self-destructive force the *flesh* or the 'sinful nature'. Some theology experts call it the 'old sin nature'. C.S. Lewis called it 'the shadowy zoo within[2].' Stephen King, writing from a non-biblical perspective, compared it to a spacecraft full of aliens landing in his brain and taking over.[3]

Some psychologists call it the 'shadow'. We'll stick with the *flesh* or your Inner Mess. For now, it's enough to recognize that many parts of your personality are dedicated to doing what Jesus wouldn't do. Meet your Inner Mess.

When life is smooth, your Inner Mess settles down. But when you face stress, trauma, loss, or any threatening condition, your characters go berserk. You might blurt out something like I did, and wonder, 'Where did that come from?' You might cross a moral boundary you swore you'd never cross: pornography, an affair, doing drugs, or gambling away the nest egg. You might push away the people you love the most. You might develop an addictive lifestyle. Or dislike yourself, or even harm yourself. It can feel so crazy, and even evil, that you sometimes wonder if you really have God in your life at all. Your Inner Mess revels in trashing your outer world.

This is why the apostle Paul's very personal lament resonates with so many followers of Jesus: 'When I want to do good, I don't. And when I try not to do wrong, I do it anyway' (Romans 7:19, NLT). I completely get that.

I'm especially relieved to know these words were written by a saint.

The Inner Mess is the source of virtually every major struggle in your life. 'Where do wars and fights come from among you? Do they not come from your desires for pleasure that war in your members?' (James 4:1). James affirms that the external conflict in your relationships flows out of the internal conflict in your soul.

He also describes your internal conflict as a 'war in your members'. Translation: the back of the bus is shooting spitballs at the front of the bus. Your 'members' are the characters on your bus, like a pack of snarling dogs. This is exactly what my wife said about me this morning. But I just snapped at her.

Now you know why sometimes you talk to yourself. Your characters are engaged in a constant shouting match, and sometimes it becomes audible. It's creepy. Your Inner Mess generates a host of malfunctions; here's a partial list:

18

- Random acts of swearing
- Losing your car keys before a date, important interview, or church service that you're being dragged to against your will
- Chronic procrastination
- Overeating and undereating
- Overachieving and underachieving
- Sarcasm and cynicism
- Superficial marriage, dating, or friendships
- Bratty behavior
- Excessive concern with appearance
- All forms of addiction: alcohol, gambling, drugs, shopping, sexual addictions, fetishism
- Pornography, affairs, crossing sexual boundaries
- Self-righteousness, judgmentalism, religious superiority
- Financial mismanagement
- Perfectionism
- A martyr's spirit
- Leading a double life
- Abusiveness, cruelty
- Self-absorption
- Indecisiveness, 'failure to launch'
- Ultimately, a shallow relationship with God.

A Failure of Containment

What is a follower of Jesus to do with the Inner Mess?

Too many Christians reply, 'Suppress those desires! Hide the struggles. Cap the anger. Slap a smile over the hatred. Be a good Christian. Contain your Inner Mess!'

None of this works.

The energy you spend on containment is your soul's equivalent of a leaky gas tank. It's draining, emotionally and spiritually. You wind up with less energy to devote to your marriage, your kids, your dating life, or your other

feel free to add to the list anything that was missed. ☺

19

relationships. You have less energy for your life's mission. The leaky tank wears you out.

Over time, your ability to contain the rowdy crowd grows weaker. You slip up more and more. Soon, others notice something wrong with you. As your dark side gains control, it becomes harder to hide. The armor cracks.

The journals of King David bear this out. After horrendous, out-of-control episodes of adultery, betrayal and abuse of power, and a murder to cover it all up, David wrote, 'When I refused to confess my sin, I was weak and miserable, and I groaned all day long' (Psalm 32:3, NLT). Containment doesn't work.

The desire to hide your Inner Mess is natural. In a weirdly sick way, it's especially natural for followers of Jesus. The Christian subculture has, by and large, rewarded those who successfully contain their Inner Mess. At the same time it has punished those who let it show. Ask the latest pastor who's fallen from grace.

That's why even devoted followers of Jesus have a tough time owning up to the harsh, dirty, self-absorbed, dangerous sides of our personalities. Christians shouldn't lean on the horn or shout curse words at other drivers, right? We shouldn't feel scary and strange impulses at times, should we?

So, rather than admit we have a dark side and deal with the uncomfortable implications of it, it seems better to just hide.

Hypocrites?
But Jesus taught that you can't hide forever:

> *Whatever you have said in the dark will be heard in the light, and what you have whispered behind closed doors will be shouted from the housetops for all to hear!*
>
> (Luke 12:3, NLT)

In this context, Jesus is judging the Pharisees for hypocrisy. The Pharisees were religious leaders. In their own eyes, they were highly successful followers of God. But to Jesus they were fakes.

Why?

Because they based their life with God on picky little procedures for every aspect of life. Follow the procedures, they implied, and God will be happy with you. So will the Pharisees. Violate the procedures, and all hell breaks loose.

To Jesus, their glaring error was how they constricted life with God. In effect, they made life with God an ongoing effort to bury the Inner Mess under a mountain of religious activity. It was less about transformation than about image.

'Hypocrites,' Jesus called them. 'Hypocrites' translates the original Greek word *hupokrites* [hoo-POK-ree-tace]. Hupokrites referred to the masks used by actors in ancient Greek drama. The Pharisees were guilty of masking the Inner Mess instead of mastering it. This is why Jesus called them 'whitewashed tombs'. They looked great on the outside, but emanated the stench of death from the inside (Matthew 23:27).

Plus, they sent a whole lot of spiritual seekers running away from God as fast as their unregenerate legs could carry them.

No matter how practiced you are at containing your Inner Mess, you will one day shout it from the rooftops. My Sunday School teachers first laid that verse on me when I was in junior high. My twelve-year-old mind pictured a cosmic TV screen with my latest sins broadcast for the entire universe to see. It scared me then. It scares me today.

Imagine shouting your deepest, most embarrassing secrets from a rooftop. Or posting them on YouTube. Or printing them in the church bulletin. Some small-town newspapers publish the names of men who have been arrested for picking up hookers. The drive to hide the Inner Mess is a powerful motivator.

My friend Tommy produced pornography before he met Jesus. He tells heartbreaking stories of young women begging him to get their pictures back. But it was too late. The rights to their pictures had been sold and the pictures had been distributed on the Internet. Their secrets were being shouted from the rooftops.

Jesus is not teaching that God broadcasts your sins to the world. <u>He's teaching that you'll do it.</u> You'll crack. You'll 'out' yourself. You can't contain your Inner Mess forever. It's only a matter of time before you slip.

And no matter how many religious practices you might observe, they cannot gloss over a life dominated by your Inner Mess. In fact, the more religious practices you pile on, the more you become a hypocrite.

• *unrepented sin will find you out.*

Reality, not Containment

The simple truth is that Christianity is a relationship with God. Like all healthy relationships, it has to be based on reality. And that includes the unpleasant realities about the nasty passengers at the back of your bus.

So when the Pharisees excelled at containing their Inner Mess and gave the impression they were closer to God – and when they taught the people to follow their religious procedures as if they had dropped down from heaven – Jesus couldn't stand it. He tore into them, not to push them away, but to blow the lid off their Inner Mess. <u>Either you relate to God with your whole self, mess and all, or you don't relate to him at all.</u>

If Jesus' death and resurrection mean anything, they mean the freedom to be real. Jesus may be the one person in your life who gives you freedom to let down your guard. He came precisely because of your Inner Mess. If you don't have an Inner Mess, he has nothing to offer you.

• Don't worry. You qualify.

I want to show you how to let Jesus finish what your first encounter with him began.

In case your Inner Saint is warning, 'I can see where this is headed – he's a libertine! Anything goes! License to sin!' you can relax. We won't go there. *God's love is not a permission slip for sin; it's the power to be whole.*

Your Inner C.I.A. Agent may sound the next alarm: 'Watch out! He'll make you blab everything to everybody! This stuff is CLASSIFIED.' You can relax too. I will not tell you to broadcast your secrets to the world. Instead, I'll guide you to gradually uncover them before God and yourself. And perhaps a trusted circle of friends. All at your own pace, when you're ready, and only if you want to.

If you long for a healthy, balanced, adventurous Christian life, you have to deal with your Inner Mess. You need permission to come out of the shadows. You need to understand Jesus' attitude toward the back of your bus.

Unfortunately, most Christians have never been equipped to deal with their Inner Mess.

Let's fix that right now, together. Let's explore the Bible's proven wisdom for bringing peace to your Inner Mess. It's time to discover how to stop your Inner Mess from trashing your outer world.

I'm not saying that I have got it all figured out or that my Inner Brat hasn't commandeered the bus lately. I'm just saying that God's ways work. As often as I follow them, my life proves it. So let's get going. Just don't do anything with this book that will make me unleash my Inner Jerk. He might have to swear at you. Or worse.

Taking Out the Trash

....

Describe a few times when you blurted out something embarrassing that you didn't plan to.

Identify some of the conflicting voices inside you. What do you tell yourself when you have failed or feel threatened?

What would you call the main character who has been driving your bus for the last couple of months? What would your spouse or closest friends call that character?

Which one personal secret would you least like to have 'shouted from the rooftops'?

Describe an episode when you demonstrated the truth of Romans 7:19, 'When I want to do good, I don't. And when I try not to do wrong, I do it anyway' (NLT).

Prayer: For complete openness and honesty with God and yourself as you face up to your own Inner Mess.

Chapter 2
Your Inner Sinner

*'If God were to justify and save only those who are pure
and upright, heaven would be empty of inhabitants.'*
Augustus Toplady, 1740–78

Scott's face lit up when he glanced at the well-worn picture
of his wife and son clipped to his visor. I do this for them, he
thought. His labor union had just negotiated a great retirement
package with the transit authority. *Hang in there, and we'll be set
for life. One day at a time,* he reminded himself.

Scott opened the bus door for a rising star from the Board
of Trade. Jason something, he remembered. He recognized
him from the newspapers. Fresh out of business school, he
was a rookie commodities trader and had made some good
moves that had paid off. Scott remembered the picture of
Jason with his knockout new wife. The article said that on most
days Jason jogged from his loft apartment on West Madison
Avenue to the exchange. But today was rainy.

Scott thought, 'Wow, there's a guy who has everything
going for him.'

He didn't have a clue how wrong he was. Jason moved
slowly. His eyes looked dull. Rain splatted against his Burberry
coat with dull thuds. He hardly noticed. He paid his fare and
found a seat in the middle of the bus.

Jason stared out the window. He couldn't believe how
close he had come to getting caught. He had just hopped out
of bed with his new assistant and was cracking a joke, when,

out of the corner of his eye, he saw something that made his blood run cold. His wife was coming up the path. What was she doing home at that time?

Panicked whispers. Hurried dressing. Quick coordination of alibis. Jason threw the covers back on the bed and straightened up the room. His assistant slipped out the back door just as Jason's wife unlocked the front door. He greeted her with a lame joke and a broken heart. He couldn't look her in the eye.

How could I have been such an idiot? She's been nothing but good to me, and I've blown it . It wasn't the first time. He prayed it would be the last. *I vowed before God and everybody to be faithful. I've let down my wife. Myself. Jesus.* He called out a hollow goodbye, threw on his coat, and hurried to the bus stop. He didn't hear his wife remind him to take an umbrella. The ache wouldn't go away.

How could he face his assistant today? He knew he should stop, but didn't have the strength. Jason stared vacantly out the bus window. I can't let her find out; she'll be crushed. I will carry this secret to my grave.

Scott inched back into the traffic. He felt unsettled. He could not wait to get home. He had no idea how much more unsettled he would feel soon.

* * *

For the flesh lusts against the Spirit, and the Spirit
against the flesh; and these are contrary to one another, so
that you do not do the things that you wish.

(Galatians 5:17)

For much of my childhood, my parents packed me off to summer camp in Wisconsin. Swimming, boating, fishing, archery, crafts, Bible stories. The camp offered 123 rolling acres of lakes, woods, creeks and frogs. All very cool to a city kid. One of the few places off limits was the garbage dump.

To a nine-year-old boy, the appeal of an off-limits garbage dump was too much to resist. It was hidden in a little valley, but there was no mistaking the smell. Old tires, machinery, broken bikes and equipment, a few rodents.

A couple of us sneaked in. We tried to shoot chipmunks with our bows and arrows. I never got one. For us boys, the garbage dump was just another playground. Too bad it was a toxic playground. A lot like the Inner Mess.

Let's define it more thoroughly:

> *Your Inner Mess ('the flesh') is the garbage dump of your soul. It is the dumping ground for your morally fallen desires, drives, thoughts, beliefs, instincts and habits – all the parts of you that resist God. Left unchecked, your Inner Mess trashes your outer world, contaminates your relationships, spoils your achievements, and makes your life stink.*

Sometimes we treat our flesh like a playground. That's because it masquerades as a party waiting to happen; as your wild and crazy part. No matter how nasty it becomes, most people simply don't see the flesh for the danger it really is. It's too easy to look past it, neglect it, or brush it off. Research indicates that not even half of born-again Americans believe that God really expects them to be holy.[1] Might we call this a self-fulfilling prophecy?

God is smart enough to recognize that a whole lot of sins are indeed fun – temporarily. He calls this 'the passing pleasure of sin' (Hebrews 11:25). The Inner Mess can indeed look more like a playground than a toxic spill. That's partly why it's so dangerous. Lurking beneath the fun stuff is a simmering cauldron of microbes and chemicals that would eat your liver if you gave it a chance.

What exactly is the Inner Mess?

To answer that, we need to sift through the garbage dump in our souls. You might want to wear rubber gloves.

Flesh vs. Body

When the Bible uses the word 'flesh' it is not referring simply to your physical body. This was a revelation for me. I grew up in an extremely conservative, fundamentalist church. We were fundamentalists and proud of it. I'm grateful for that little church and for my spiritual mentors. They taught me a lot, and I knew I was loved.

But I also had a lot of unlearning to do.

My church confused the flesh with the body. They implied that my physical drives were somehow dirty. When God warned against the lusts of the flesh, that translated as the desires of my body. So, for example, since 'rock and roll' appealed to the body, rock music was out. So were drums.

God was anti-body.

This teaching produced all sorts of weirdness in me. I wanted to please God, and since the number-one body-related sin was sex, I was hyper-careful about the opposite sex. I was careful not to look at girls' bodies, just their faces. I was careful not to touch, hold hands, hug, or kiss. One of my junior-high Sunday-school teachers emphasized a verse that says, 'It is good for a man not to touch a woman' (1 Corinthians 7:1, KJV). Never mind that the context and the original Greek are simply authorizing celibacy as a way of life. For us, it meant no dating and hands off.

These things were out of bounds because bodily pleasure was taboo. If a girl touched me, even innocently, I broke into a cold sweat. I didn't want to date because that would be the first step toward indulging my flesh.

It was the same with dancing. They implied it was 'a vertical expression of a horizontal desire'.

Meanwhile, every hormone in my adolescent body was driving me in the opposite direction. I was like a car with both the brake pedal and the gas pedal pressed to the floor. Smoke billowed out from under the hood. Something had to give. Thankfully, it did – and in a healthy way.

28

Some time during my high-school years, my uncle gave me an audio sermon by a pastor he liked. The pastor pointed out that, just as the Bible uses the word 'heart' in a non-physical, non-literal way, it also uses the word 'flesh' in a non-physical, non-literal way. Neither word refers to bodily organs. Ancient people used body parts to describe functions of thinking and feeling. Biblical terms such as 'kidneys' or 'bowels' were not literal, but referred to passionate emotions.[2]

Later on I found out that the whole idea that my bodily flesh was evil was a false teaching that came from the dualism of Greek philosophers.

Whatever the Bible meant by 'the flesh', it wasn't exactly my body. It affected my body. It distorted the appetites of my body. The flesh could even use my body as an instrument of evil. But my body itself was not evil. 'Flesh' did not equal 'body'.

The lights came on.

I discovered that when God created Adam and Eve, he declared them to be 'very good' (Genesis 1:31). That included their bodies. When the psalmist claimed to be 'fearfully and wonderfully made', he was referring to his body (Psalm 139:14). I came to believe that my body was good, morally speaking (my physique was another matter). I didn't understand it all, but for the first time I was able to separate my flesh (the garbage dump in my soul) from my body.

God is pro-body and anti-flesh.

I immediately became huggable. And touchable. One of my church friends even commented, 'How come you're hugging everybody now?' I just smiled.

But I still can't dance.

So if the flesh isn't my physical body, then what is it?

It is the part of you that says, 'Sometimes I want to be bad.'

Sometimes I Want to Be Bad

In eleven places, the Bible describes the function of the flesh using the word 'lust' or 'desire' — for example, the common phrase 'the lust of the flesh' (2 Peter 2:18; 1 John 2:16). Or the Bible says that your 'flesh lusts' against the Spirit (Galatians 5:16). To lust simply means to have a strong desire, to want something badly.

Whatever else your flesh may be, it is a part of you that wants stuff badly. Your Inner Mess is a collection of strong desires and drives. Specifically, the flesh is a collection of morally corrupt strong desires and drives. Yes, some of these desires and drives are bodily appetites: food, pleasure, sex, comfort. But those desires themselves are not necessarily evil; it depends on how you fulfill them.

Fleshly desires can be physical, mental, spiritual, or emotional.

My friend Chris wears a tee shirt that says, 'Sometimes I like to be bad.' As Chris says, it's nothing to be proud of, but it's true. Those bad 'likes' constitute your Inner Mess. Sometimes parts of you (your Inner Mess) want to be bad.

What about decent, churchgoing Christians?

During a question-and-answer period in a sermon on the Inner Mess, I asked my church about it. I asked them to help me list desires and drives that God doesn't want for our lives. As people called out their answers, I wrote them on a giant marker board.

Here's what we came up with:

Desires and Drives That God Doesn't Want for Our Lives

• stealing • lying • hitting
• killing • adultery • pre-marital sex • pornography
• revenge • sexual carousing
• murder • violence • illegal drugs
• fetishism • alcoholism • hatred

At this point we noticed a pattern. We were only listing 'bad' sins that other people do (we thought). So I asked the group

30

to concentrate on subtle sins, or religious sins, or on sins that were generally tolerated among church people.

Here is our second list:

Desires and Drives That Christians Overlook or Accept

- phoniness • hypocrisy • arrogance
- self-righteousness • slander • pretending to be perfect
- perfectionism • materialism • backbiting
- gossip • judging/casting stones • not helping the poor
- being critical while claiming to be constructive
- pretending to pray more than you do
- pretending to love God more than you do
- pretending not to have the struggles you do

After making our two lists, we opened our Bibles to Galatians 5:19 only to discover a very similar catalog called 'the works of the flesh'.

> *Now the works of the flesh are evident, which are: adultery, fornication, uncleanness, lewdness, idolatry, sorcery, hatred, contentions, jealousies, outbursts of wrath, selfish ambitions, dissensions, heresies, envy, murders, drunkenness, revelries, and the like; of which I tell you beforehand, just as I also told you in time past, that those who practice such things will not inherit the kingdom of God.*

(Galatians 5:19–21)

We were surprised at how similar our lists were to the Bible's. The works of the flesh are 'evident'.

It was time to lower the hammer on my church. 'Church,' I announced in a somber pastor-voice, 'I want you to know something about me: see all those sins we've listed? I want that stuff.' I paused to let my confession sink in. 'Your pastor,' I confessed, 'wants to be bad.'

31

Only a few eyebrows were raised. They weren't surprised. In fact, most people in my church were relieved that I could admit it. My Inner Mess was no surprise to them. And I thought I was letting them in on some big secret.

Even Followers of Jesus

You might argue, 'Bill, Christians don't want evil things. We don't desire the works of the flesh. I don't want that stuff. In fact, I want the opposite. I want to be holy. I want to be good. I want to follow God's plan for my life. I don't want to operate according to my Inner Mess.'

Oh yes you do! Have you ever considered the possibility that denying your Inner Mess only makes it worse?

Tim was a lanky, sandy-haired, easy-going, blue-collar guy. He had recently started attending church again and had received Jesus as his Savior. We were sitting on a small boat, fishing for bass on a cool spring day. He was telling me how much he wanted to follow Jesus faithfully. I believed him. Tim shared that he was dating a Christian woman in our church and wanted to do things right this time. He didn't want to get sexually active, as he had done in his previous relationships. I applauded that.

Tim said, 'Bill, I really don't want to have sex with her.'

I said, 'You're a liar.' Tim looked shocked and wounded.

Nice pastor, huh? Tim stuttered a little.

His eyes squinted.

'Bill, I'm sincere. I mean it. I even told Jen I didn't want to have sex with her and that I wanted our relationship to please God.' He looked genuinely proud. He wanted me to congratulate him.

I looked at Tim, smiled, and offhandedly suggested, 'Then you're both a liar and a manipulator.' I'm sure he felt very close to me at that moment. 'Tim, don't say you don't want to have sex with Jen. Of course you do. I know you. You know you. It's a natural desire. You want to have sex with her, so don't deny it.

'I also believe that another part of you really wants to wait. You have both drives going on, right?'

Tim grinned and nodded yes.

'Okay, so when you told Jen that you didn't want to have sex with her, at least part of that was a lie, right?' Tim agreed.

But I wasn't done yet.

'It gets worse,' I whispered, making him lean in to me. 'By lying to Jen about not wanting to have sex with her, you probably accomplished two objectives: you made her feel even more attracted to you, right?'

He grinned again and agreed.

'Plus you got her to drop her defenses. That makes you a manipulator,' I concluded.

Tim's jaw dropped. He sat back. Then he smiled. And we had a great reality check about Inner Mess desires and drives.

Tim was denying his very real internal conflict. He was denying that his flesh lusted against God's Spirit. To cap it all, he was making that denial in the name of Jesus. Just imagine all the Christian weirdness and instability this created for his relationship. With his mouth he said, 'I don't want to have sex with you.' But with everything else, he oozed seduction.

I suggested, 'A better way to have that conversation is to admit, "Jen, I'm attracted to you, and there's a part of me that wants to go further than God wants us to go. But there's another part of me, a better part of me, that wants to do things God's way. So let's be really careful and alert to these temptations, okay? Let's both keep up our guard."'

The Inner Mess can weasel its way into even the noblest of intentions. That's why it is so healthy to refer to yourself as a collection of parts. Try it; it's cathartic.

A part of me wants to sit down in front of the TV and eat two pints of Chunky Monkey ice cream. But a better part of me chooses something a little more healthy.

Part of me wants to indulge in some juicy gossip. But a better part of me wants to keep my mouth shut.

Part of me wants to look at porn. Or have an affair. But a better part of me chooses to be loyal to my spouse, my family and God.

Part of me wants to be emperor of the world. But a better part of me knows what a hassle that would be. Plus, the saner parts of me know I'm not worthy.

I want that crazy stuff, and even worse stuff. This is why the Bible tags all of us as sinners. Given the opportunity, any one of us could commit just about any sin. I am a sinner from the inside out.

All of those parts of me – those morally fallen, depraved, indulgent, self-absorbed, arrogant, critical, superficial, hyper-religious parts of me – are passengers on my bus. Mini-me's. Say hello to my Inner Mess. Feeling superior yet? Don't. Your Inner Mess might be more polished, but it's just as corrupt as mine.

I'm not saying that all our desires are bad. We are complex beings. Many of our desires – in fact the majority of them – can be quite good. They can even align perfectly with God's desires. Tim and Jen both had a set of very godly desires for their relationship. The problem was that they denied an equally real, but sordidly opposite, set of sinful desires. That denial is dangerous.

Admitting that I want bad stuff doesn't negate all the good stuff. It's just telling the unpleasant truth.

A Terrible, Horrible, No-Good, Very Bad Choice

So why did God make us this way? Answer: he didn't. When you get to heaven, you might want to have a few words with Adam. Your Inner Mess is a 'gift' from him. It went something like this:

EVE (wiping her chin): Hon, this is sooooo juicy.
ADAM: I can't believe you did that! You are totally busted!

EVE: It's worth it! You gotta taste this stuff. Here, just smell it.

ADAM: No way! I'm not even getting close to it.

EVE (abruptly screaming): I SAID SMELL IT RIGHT NOW, MISTER!

ADAM: Okay, okay! I'll smell it. Just quit screaming at me. That's not like you.

EVE (suddenly calm): Oh, was I screaming? Something's happening to me. I feel strange. Like there's another voice in me, or something.

ADAM (smelling the fruit): Wow! That does smell delicious!

EVE (smiling): I told you so. Want a bite?

ADAM: I already told you, I'm not going to do it.

EVE (abruptly crying): You don't love me any more, do you? If I'd had a mother, she would have warned me about you. (sobbing)

ADAM: Okay, okay. Shhhh. That's all right, honey. Don't cry. (puts his arm around her) Here, just give me one little bite.

EVE (happy): Really? Oooooh. I am so turned on right now...

The rest is history.

Without going into the justice of it all, let's just recognize that the Inner Mess is part of the price we pay for being members of a fallen race. We inherited it from our father, Adam, Bible scholars say that the propensity to sin ('I want bad stuff') is transmitted down our family tree from Adam, the original sinner. The human race brought this on itself. We can't blame God.

When Adam sinned, in effect, we all sinned. His sin introduced a moral twist into our very beings (Romans 5:12–21). Sometimes this is called 'original sin' or 'inherited sin' or 'transmitted sin'. Earlier generations of Christians called it a 'corruption of nature', the 'sinful nature', or the 'old sin nature'. I'll stick with the flesh or the Inner Mess. Whatever term you choose, it's all courtesy of Adam and his terrible, horrible, no-good, very bad choice.

[handwritten margin note: Thanks Adam! Now I must choose to obey God and the Holy Spirit in me. But that is ok Because He said He will always be there with Me]

But don't be too hard on Adam. Every day you prove that, if you had been in his bare feet, you would have made the same choice.

It's time to collectively confess our dirty little Christian secret. Want to join me? Raise your right hand and repeat after me: I have desires and drives that are morally fallen and displeasing to God and I struggle with them all the time. I have a very big, very smelly Inner Mess. I'm a sinner, and I want bad stuff.

There, don't you feel better now? Confession is the first step in bringing peace to your Inner Mess.

But don't go snapping off those rubber gloves, or unzipping those overalls just yet. We're hardly up to our wrists in the garbage dump in our souls.

My Flesh — I want — I need — I think I should — This will please God — There's nothing wrong with that — why can't I? — I should have — I deseve that. The flesh will always be looking for a way to feed itself. So I think we need to fill our soul up with God's Holy Spirit Provided food. Re: The life that is in Jesus Himself — He is the bread of life, and the resurrection. Fill me up Lord!

Taking Out the Trash

Do you believe that a truly holy life is possible? Why or why not? To what degree?

What have been the three most damaging desires or habits that have influenced your family tree? What are the three most damaging desires or habits that influence your life?

Before you picked up this book, what came to mind when you heard the words *flesh, carnal,* or *carnality*?

Describe a time when you've denied – to yourself, God, or somebody else – an embarrassing truth about yourself.

When was the last time you felt *torn*? Practice describing yourself as a collection of parts. For example: 'Part of me wants to numb my pain through eating [drinking, sex, workaholism, etc.] but another part of me knows that would be unhealthy.'

What does 1 John 1:8 say about denying sin in our lives? 'If we say that we have no sin, we deceive ourselves, and the truth is not in us.'

Prayer: For insight into the depths of your own Inner Mess.

Chapter 3
Your Inner Saint

'A proud faith is as much a contradiction as a humble devil.'

Stephen Charnock, 1628–1680

Scott tried to drive with just the left wiper running. The attempt was vain; it was raining too hard. With a sigh, he flipped on the right wiper. The blades were not in sync with each other. This annoyed him. It also annoyed many of his passengers, and they were already on edge.

The bus was mostly empty. Scott was glad. Rain always slowed down traffic, and today was no exception. *I'll be way behind schedule*, he thought. Regulations permitted him to be behind schedule. He'd get into trouble only if he were ahead of schedule – something few riders realized. They would be late for work, and they would blame him. *Why didn't you get out of bed a little earlier? You knew it was going to rain.*

The bus belched as he slanted in for his next passenger. The door opened for a woman wearing a dark-blue polyester blazer with a matching skirt. The hem fell four inches below her knees. She wore black shoes, sturdy and functional. A perfectly formed bun perched high atop her head. She snapped her umbrella shut, stepped on board and flicked a speck of lint from her lapel. Scott noticed her pro-life lapel pin.

He forced a smile.

'The Lord bless you,' she said as she handed Scott her transfer. With the transfer was a small piece of literature. A 'tract', she had once called it. She was always handing out tracts. Most of the riders didn't care. But Scott worried that some of today's riders might. He forced another smile.

Scott shifted positions and accepted the tract without comment. She eyed him up and down, her face registering disapproval. 'Read it. It will show you how to put your life in order,' she instructed.

His nod was polite but non-committal.

It's not that Scott was unreligious. He just didn't know this lady, and she didn't know him. Who was she to tell him how to get his life in order? It looked to Scott as if her life could use some ordering. She came across as pushy – as if she was trying to sell him something.

He watched in the mirror as the tract lady moved toward the rear. The riders who had seen her before avoided eye contact. Who wanted to be preached at for the next hour?

She pursed her lips when she saw the tattooed felon. Her chin tilted up ever so slightly. She looked down at him. Out came a barely perceptible, but definitely audible, sniff. A woman on a mission, the lady in blue chose the seat across the aisle from him. She sat erect, searching her handbag for just the right tract. The felon had endured life on the streets and behind bars, but nothing in his experience had prepared him for the tract lady.

Scott shook his head as he swung the bus back into the traffic, its wipers thumping their uneven beat.

* * *

> *These things indeed have an appearance of wisdom in self-imposed religion, false humility, and neglect of the body, but are of no value against the indulgence of the flesh*

> (Colossians 2:23).

As the whip came down on his back, Dominic winced in

The Staunch tract lady.

pain. But he did not cry out. He lifted his hand, and deftly swung the whip again, wrapping it around his body with a crack. Dominic was reading the Psalms – all 150 of them. It would take weeks, but he was obsessed. For each psalm, he brought down the lash one hundred times. Penance for a year of misdeeds. He made his back an open wound. St. Dominic Loricatus believed in the mortification of the flesh. And he practiced what he preached.

The Catholic Church condemned the practice of self-flagellation in A.D. 1261, but not before it had gained a decent following. Known as Flagellants, followers of St. Dominic paraded through towns, swinging whips across their backs. They believed that this was the only way to 'put to death' the deeds of the flesh (Colossians 3:5). Flagellants marched in Italy, Austria, and Germany.

The Flagellant movement quickly faded out. I imagine they had a tough time with recruitment.

Other self-injuring practices became popular. St. Dominic Loricatus took his name from the *lorica*, a rough, chain-mail undershirt worn against his skin. The constant discomfort was intended to demotivate his Inner Mess. Others wore camel-hair shirts – scratchy and irritating. Some stared into the sun. Some went on long fasts from food and water. Others slept on rocks, the more uncomfortable the better. Still others crawled on hands and knees up long, stone stairways.

Looking back from today's vantage point, it's not my place to condemn these people. In many ways, I admire them. I completely disagree with their methods and I reject their underlying beliefs, but I admire their devotion. They had guts.

But they didn't have true wisdom on how to handle the Inner Mess. The Bible warns that in these cases, no matter how wise, religious, humble, or even self-sacrificial our practices may be, they are of 'no value against the indulgence of the flesh' (Colossians 2:23).

The whips and hair shirts may have disappeared, but

the spirit that inspired them has not. Unfortunately for the Flagellants and their modern-day counterparts, Colossians 2:23 affirms that <u>no human effort can overturn the flesh's domination.</u>

But does that stop us from trying? Here are five tried and failed non-solutions to our Inner Mess predicament.

Guilt-trip It

I mentioned before that I was reared in a fundamentalist church. For my first twenty years, that small church was the center of my life. We were frozen in time: classic hymns sung to an organ, suits and ties, potluck dinners, hard-backed pews, church picnics, and a general distrust of 'the world out there'. My church was a cocoon from the big bad world.

I knew that I was loved. I was wanted. I was safe.

I was also guilty. I couldn't help myself. I was constantly breaking God's law, and my church made sure I knew it. My conscience worked overtime. Yes, I knew that Jesus had paid for my sins. But I never grasped how fully.

So I always had something to feel guilty about. I didn't obey my parents enough. I didn't love Jesus enough. I didn't control my lustful thoughts enough. I didn't abstain from worldly pleasure enough. Going to movies was taboo. When I saw *Star Wars* for the first time, I couldn't completely relax, even though I loved the movie. I felt dirty just sitting in a movie theater.

Growing up fundamentalist is like sitting in a dentist's chair: I sat with a death-grip on the handles, just waiting for the high-pitched drill to touch the soft, sensitive core.

I was my own harshest critic. My Inner Judge repeatedly slammed his gavel and condemned me. The voices inside my head hissed that I was a moral failure. <u>I developed a groveling kind of spirituality.</u> I felt worthless before God. A member of our youth group wrote a song about it:

I wake up every morning, at the break of day.
Stand before the bathroom mirror,
Look at myself and say: I am a worm.
I'm lowdown, good for nothing at all.
I don't walk down the street, I crawl.
I only feel about two feet tall.
And everyone's better than me.

Well, after I say that forty times
I walk on down the street.
My hands in my pockets, my head hanging low,
My eyes staring at my feet:
Please step on me!

Rob me, bruise me, scorn me, use me!
It's good for me when you abuse me!
Tie me to a bomb and fuse me!
I won't put up a fight.[1]

That song expresses the kind of self-deprecating guilt I heaped on myself during my formative years. I don't believe my church intended this – it was the unintended by-product of a desire to keep us kids on the straight and narrow, combined with some unhealthy emotional factors that I brought to the table. The result was a toxic guilt-gravy poured over my Inner Mess.

What I didn't know then was that my guilt was the equivalent of an inner whipping. And it was unnecessary because of Jesus.

To round out my weirdness, I was actually proud of my guilt. It proved that I was morally superior to my neighbor, who – though he committed even worse sins than I – didn't have the decency to feel horrible about them.

No amount of self-inflicted guilt ever stopped my Inner Mess from trashing my outer world. 'It was of no value against the indulgence of the flesh.' So my Inner Saint did what any self-respecting church-person would do: it piled even more weight onto the burden of self-punishment. *Matt. 11:28-31 Help*

Atone For It

I refrained from drinking, dancing, swearing (mostly), playing cards, and movies (mostly). I sacrificed dating, the prom, lust, and sex. I sacrificed any college or career choice that was outside the Christian bubble. This roster of 'sacrifices-I-made-for-Jesus' defined me. It defined a whole generation of Christians. It also scared off a whole generation of non-Christians.

I also sacrificed large amounts of time. By my early college years, I was working as a produce clerk in a large grocery store. I worked the graveyard shift on weekends – 10:00 p.m. until 7:00 a.m. on Thursday, Friday, and Saturday.

After working all night Saturday and into Sunday morning, I grabbed a quick breakfast and headed straight to church. I helped set up chairs. I played the piano (amateurishly) for our worship service. Then I went home for a quick nap. Then back to church on Sunday night for another round of worship.

Tuesday night I ran the boys' club. Wednesday night I joined the prayer meeting. Thursday night I drove my sister and her friends to our church's girls' club. I stayed to help. Then I drove them home. And went straight to work. Friday night I helped with the youth group, and then went to work. And started my week over again.

Dating? No time for it; I was busy serving the Almighty. Plus, since I had mastery over my flesh, I didn't need it.

I also sacrificed my ego: I knocked on doors to trick people into conversations about Jesus. I passed out tracts to strangers at O'Hare airport. I was mortified and embarrassed every minute. I'm sure God does use these methods of outreach, just not through me.

out of touch with God's will.

We even made a hero out of one church leader who boasted that he was 'busy for Jesus' at church while his wife was in the hospital delivering their first child.

Christianity's finest hour.

We were pedaling as fast as we could.

Why did we make these sacrifices? I can't speak for

anybody else, but I know why I did: I was sacrificing myself so that God would forgive my backlog of sins. I criticized the theological position that required penance. What I didn't realize was that my whole life was a penance.

There is a time and a place for self-sacrifice. It is an essential part of keeping faith with God. However, when we use self-sacrifice to atone for the sins of our Inner Mess, God is not pleased. Your Inner Mess can never atone for your Inner Mess. But don't underestimate its willingness to try.

Not Understanding what Christ Accomplished on the cross.

Underestimate It

I hadn't seen Daniel for months, so I wasn't ready for how much he had changed. Daniel served as the pastor in a medium-sized church near mine. When he approached me after a worship service, I hardly recognized him. He looked thin. Gaunt. His eyes looked dull. There was something terribly wrong. I thought he was sick. Daniel forced a smile as he spoke.

'I guess you already heard.'

'Heard what?'

'Nobody told you?' He tilted his head as if he didn't believe me.

'Told me what? What's going on?' My jaw was tense.

Daniel let out a long sigh. 'I had an affair. I cheated on my wife. And I had to resign from my church.'

He slumped there, barely making eye contact.

I felt as if I'd just been kicked in the gut.

We met at a coffee shop the next day. As Daniel's story unfolded, my heart ached.

One phrase jumped out at me, because Daniel repeated it over and over: 'Bill, I was sure this was the one sin I could never do.'

'I never thought I could do this.'

Daniel had underestimated his Inner Mess, a miscalculation that devastated his outer world. He proved the truth of the Bible's warning: 'Therefore let him who thinks he stands take heed lest he fall' (1 Corinthians 10:12).

Answer this question with brutal honesty: What would you do if you were one hundred per cent certain you'd never get caught? As one old-time preacher told his church, 'If you knew the corruption that was in my heart, you wouldn't waste your time listening to me.' Then he paused and added, 'But that's okay. If I knew the corruption in your hearts, I wouldn't waste my time preaching to you.'

Daniel discovered the corruption in his heart the hard way. He and his wife are rebuilding their family; I hope they make it. Consider this book a golden opportunity to discover your equally depraved corruption the easy way.

I'm inviting you to unflinchingly acknowledge your Inner Mess: to own up to each superficial, ugly, distorted, dangerous, self-absorbed potential within you. Until you make a realistic appraisal of your Inner Mess, you'll never be free. At the end of this chapter, I'll suggest how you can get started.

Punish It

I calculate that I have lost over 650 pounds. Total. In 25-pound gain–loss cycles over the last twenty years.

To all my skinny friends who have looked down their petite noses and 'lovingly' suggested, 'Why don't you just watch what you eat?' I say, 'Thank you so much for that thought; it had never occurred to me before. Excuse me now, while I binge on Chubby Hubby ice cream until I have stomach cramps. Oh, how I want to be just like you, so I can master my Inner Mess too!'

Your Inner Mess wants you fat. Or gaunt. Or anything but healthy. In the world of the flesh, any self-destructive tendency will do.

Your flesh is its own harshest critic. In a weird way, your Inner Saint (the fake one, the pharisaical one) is dedicated to punishing your Inner Mess. It practices a twisted form of self-atonement and continually spins off new ways to trash your outer world.

At the risk of feeding your denial by overlooking your particular tendency, here is a partial, incomplete, imperfect list of flesh-induced self-punishment techniques. This list might not include you, but hopefully includes behaviors that remind you of behaviors that include you. [Yes, your flesh is that sneaky.]

Thoughts of suicide, attempts at suicide, overeating, undereating, wrecking relationships, procrastination, not following through on successful ventures, dropping out (of school, relationships, jobs, opportunities), moving from place to place before you start being successful, addictions, poor financial management, overachieving, underachieving, perfectionism, abusiveness, shallow relationships, serial marriages to the wrong kind of person, disorganization, alcoholism, excessive gambling, promiscuity, one-night stands, high-risk sex, cheating on your spouse, keeping up with the Joneses, drug abuse, anorexia, bulimia, workaholism, smoking, chewing, 'churchaholism' – it's an endless list.

Your Inner Mess insists that you pay for the misdeeds your Inner Mess creates. Eerie, if you ask me. But, no matter how much we punish ourselves, something inside us screams that it's not working. Your Inner Mess won't roll over and play dead just because it inflicts a few punishments here or there.

Perhaps if you engage it head on, you might find victory.

Fight It

Steve's finger hesitated over the mouse button. One click and his favorite porn site would materialize before his eyes. His heart pounded. He knew he should be investing in real relationships with real women. He knew he was only feeding an industry that exploited vulnerable women. He knew that porn was wrong. He knew it all.

No! This time I won't give in.

Jesus Allready Paid the Price for our Sin. Accept God's Grace + Mercy.

He pushed back his chair and went to the fridge for a beer. *I can stop this. I'm better than this. I could be out dating. Bonding. Building a life with a real, flesh-and- blood woman. No. I'm finished with porn. I'm not going to use it again.*

God, give me strength.

Back in his office, he switched off his computer. As the screen went black, Steve reached for his Bible and flipped through it. Nothing jumped out at him.

His eyes glazed over. He was frustrated. *I'm going to snap.*

Steve grabbed the remote and flipped on the TV. Reruns. He turned it off.

God, where are you?

The computer sounded its familiar startup tune as Steve flipped it back on. He couldn't tell if his feeling was relief or resignation. He licked his lips and typed in the location. *Click…*

Tears rolled down Sally's cheeks as she felt her baby move. Her large belly signaled that she would soon become a mother. She loved her baby. *I'm never alone. I always have someone with me. I talk to her. I pray for her. I would do anything for her.*

Then why can't I stop smoking? Sally had begun smoking in junior high. Her friend Angie had egged her on. Alone in the schoolyard, in that hidden corner where the building jutted out, Sally accepted Angie's offer and took her first drag. She fought back a fit of coughing. *Why would anybody do this?*

Soon she was hooked.

None of the news about health effects deterred her. Posters of wrinkle-faced, toothless smokers only fed her denial. Even cost wasn't a factor. She worked up to a pack-a-day habit. She didn't care.

But all of that changed in the bathroom, when the ivory-colored plastic stick confirmed her suspicion. *I'm pregnant. I've got to stop smoking – if not for myself, at least for my child.*

She tried everything: going cold turkey, patches, gum. She asked her church friend Bonnie to pray for her. Nothing worked.

Sally hated herself for doing it. *This is my last one*, she told herself for the hundredth time. She struck the match…

In the early 1980s the U.S. government unveiled the slogan of its new anti-drug campaign: 'Just say no!' If kids would put the slogan into practice, drug use would decline. In theory.

I'm not going to offer an opinion on the U.S. government's war on drugs.

But I will offer an opinion about the Inner Mess: while you do have to say 'no' to your Inner Mess, that alone is not enough.

Your Inner Saint might object: 'Oh yes it is! God tells us to say "no" to "ungodliness and worldly lusts" (Titus 2:12). That's enough for me. I warned you that this guy was giving us permission to sin.'

Take a moment to remind your Inner Saint of the last habit you tried to break by just saying no. Remember Paul's consternation: 'What I hate, that I do' (Romans 7:15). Sounds as if 'just say no' didn't always work for him.

That's why my five-year-old daughter recently asked me, 'Daddy, why does your tummy stick out?' And my four-year-old son giggled as he observed, 'Daddy, your butt wiggles.' Thanks, kids. I blame you. Who can 'just say no' to a gooey sausage and pepperoni deep-dish pizza? Especially when your adorable kids wear you out and all you look forward to is a relaxing meal?

I can't drink alcohol. I mean, I'm not supposed to. It never bothered me until I was told by my church organization that I couldn't. I do not view drinking as a sin. Nowhere does the Bible condemn the responsible, occasional, moderate use of alcohol by adults. Even so, I've been told that I must abstain.

Drinking was never a problem for me. When I was eight or nine, my truck-driving, bartending dad let me have a swig of his beer, and I hated it. I was cured. He's a very wise man. At my aunt's wedding, he let me try the wine. I hated that too.

By my teens and twenties, my total consumption of alcoholic beverages (not counting cold remedies) could fit into a paper cup. Somewhere during my mid-thirties I developed a slight taste for beer — as in three or four a year. But that's it. So my desire for alcoholic beverages has always been next to nothing.

That all changed when I joined a church denomination that requires its pastors to abstain from alcoholic beverages.

I signed the pledge. I did so with full understanding and eyes wide open.

I'm not complaining, just confessing.

I understand the rationale for our policy: many of our church's families have been devastated by alcohol. We see it every day. Our denomination wants to stand against the societal flow of Mr. Booze. I get that.

But what I didn't get was the effect this modern-day 'prohibition' would have on me, a virtual teetotaler: it makes me want beer and wine more than ever before.

One hot Saturday afternoon, after I'd mowed the lawn, I popped open a Diet Pepsi, and whined to my wife that I would love an ice-cold beer right now but couldn't have one. She laughed and said, 'You don't even like beer!'

I was ticked off because I couldn't drink something I hardly ever wanted to drink. Drinking was never a problem for me until I started to fight it. Until I forced myself to 'just say no.' That's when the battle began.

Call this the unintended consequence of fighting the Inner Mess. The more you fight it, the more it trashes your outer world. Fighting the flesh actually stimulates the flesh to want what it wants even more.

This experience helped me understand some otherwise puzzling biblical statements, such as 'the strength of sin is the law' (1 Corinthians 15:56), or 'the law brings about wrath' (Romans 4:15). Translation: You can't go nose to nose with your Inner Mess and win. Your flesh wins round after round.

Why?

Because even if your grim determination or church-based laws can temporarily scare straight the characters at the back of your bus, you still haven't transformed them. Your Inner Felon is still felonious. Your Inner Blasphemer is still blasphemous. Your Inner Brat is still bratty. You're just smothering them for a while.

You need transformation. Not legislation; not determination.

Or you can keep on doing it the old-fashioned way: attend a church that outlaws dancing, drinking, and movies. Make sure that all the women wear culottes or 'skorts'. While you're at it, join the local chapter of the Temperance Union. Or buy a whip and join the Flagellants. Or join the Temperate Fundamentalist Flagellants.

Go ahead, dress your Inner Saint in the most self-deprecating armor, mount her on the steed with best fundamentalist pedigree, arm her with proper self-flagellating weaponry. Wage war against the flesh.

My money's on the Inner Mess every time.

Pedaling Up the Wrong Hill

If guilt-tripping it, atoning for it, underestimating it, punishing it, and fighting it have 'no value against the indulgence of the flesh', then why do so many Christians persist in these non-solutions?

My hunch is because that's all we've ever been taught. Oh, I'm sure that our churches teach about the power of Jesus and the Holy Spirit. Even so, the message that most Christ-followers overwhelmingly hear is the one that says 'try harder'.

Pedal faster.

But what if the real problem isn't that we're not pedaling fast enough, but that we're pedaling up the wrong hill? I hope you're open to the possibility that most of your perceptions about dealing with the Inner Mess are themselves Inner

Mess-spawned delusions. It could be that your flesh has been steering you up the wrong hill for years.

One of the first turns toward the right hill is *awareness*. Do you have even the slightest clue about the sinister menagerie lurking at the back of your bus?

Here is some practical help. You're invited to visit our online Inner Mess community at www.innermess.com. There, you can give names to your characters and you can describe how they affect your life. Anonymously. Secretly. No charge.

You'll also gain insights as you read other people's stories and share your own. Hopefully, you'll see that you're not alone. You might even root out a few Inner Mess characters that you didn't know you had.

Plus, you'll help other followers of Jesus put names to some of the dark forces in their own hearts.

If your Inner *Saint* vomits this much trash into your outer world, imagine what your Inner *Jerk* can do. I'm not ready yet. I need a nice, frosty beer first.

Root beer.

Taking Out the Trash

··

Have you ever encountered present-day counterparts of the Flagellants – those who punish themselves to atone for their sins? Where have you encountered them and how did they punish themselves?

Can you relate to growing up in an extremely conservative church? Do you know others who have grown up in an ultra-strict kind of faith? In your experience, how does that upbringing affect a person's life?

Describe two or three specific cases in which you have *underestimated* the power of your Inner Mess. What might you do differently the next time you're faced with a similar temptation?

What are the two or three most common techniques you use to *punish* your Inner Mess?

How strange does it feel to you to think that God might not want you to *fight* your flesh? What have you always believed about this? How well has a 'just say no' policy worked for you in fighting your flesh? Give some specific examples.

In Matthew 23:26, 27, what does Jesus teach about the value of external religious observances?

Prayer: For grace-induced transformation from the inside out.

Chapter 4

Your Inner Jerk

*'Most of God's people are contented to be saved from the
hell that is without; they are not so anxious to be saved
from the hell that is within.'*

Robert Murray M'Cheyne, 1813–43

Construction signs spelled trouble for Scott. Traffic slowed
and stopped as drivers squeezed into one lane. A few
disgusted drivers leaned on their horns. *That only makes it worse,*
Scott thought. He poured black coffee from a thermos into
a stainless-steel travel mug. His bus was now two-thirds full.
*Morning rush hour on a rainy day. Can't wait to finish my shift. God,
let it be easy.*

He glanced at his passengers in his rearview mirror. Some
craned their necks to see why the traffic had stopped. A middle-
aged couple on the left side, halfway back, was arguing. The
woman kept shaking her head and looking out the window.
She fought back tears. She couldn't bring herself to look at
the man next to her. Scott felt sorry for her.

The man leaned toward her. Veins stood out on his neck
and his blotchy face blushed from a hangover. He spoke in
loud whispers, but couldn't mask his disgust and anger. Words
poured forth in a stream of hisses jumbled with curses. His
arms jerked in time with his words. The woman kept her face
toward the window and shut her eyes hard. She couldn't stop
the tears from squeezing through.

Most passengers looked away. The man pressed his body

against the woman's. He elbowed her hard to punctuate his tirade. His thin lips drew back from yellowed teeth in a snarl as his voice rose, assaulting the whole bus with a torrent of curses and insults.

The woman's shoulders shook with muffled sobs.

The bag lady's lips moved in a silent debate with her inner demons.

The tract lady clucked disapproval. Her voice rose above the rain drumming on the roof of the bus. 'You watch your language, sir! There are ladies present.'

His head snapped in her direction. 'It ain't none of your business.' Bloodshot eyes squinted at her. 'Juss mind your own bizniss.' Alcohol slurred his speech. Scott had smelled it on both of them when they boarded. More sobbing.

Scott locked the air brakes and stood up. *Better get control of the situation.* He'd broken up his fair share of fights, and knew enough not to wait.

This time someone else did it for him.

'All of you… SHUT UP!' The felon's voice rattled as if there was gravel in his throat. He faced the surly drunk. 'Not one more word. I'm warning you.' He locked eyes with the man. The man sized him up and looked away. The woman grabbed his arm and pleaded with him to shut up.

The tract lady clenched her jaw. Jason pulled out a newspaper. The bag lady continued her silent dialogue. Scott waited for a moment and sat down. Traffic crept forward. *Can't wait for my shift to end.*

A belch of air released the brakes. The bus started rolling. Someone pounded furiously on the door. Scott looked out and rolled his eyes. *Can it get any worse?*

* * *

The Jerk In Me

You can be a jerk, right? Come on, tell the truth. Even if you are not as mean as the drunk guy on Scott's bus, you know that you are capable of hurting the very people you should love the most.

Sam came to me devastated. Cheryl, his wife of eleven years, had just confessed to a yearlong affair. While serving as a volunteer for an up-and-coming Christian band, she'd fallen in love with the lead singer. At Cheryl's request, Sam had opened their home to this band when they traveled through town. Sam fed the band and shared his home with them. He never intended to share his wife.

Or his bed. When Sam was at work and his kids were at school, his wife was in bed with the singer. Sam's bed. The marital bed. On and off for a year.

I talked with Cheryl. She was mildly repentant and didn't grasp the enormity of her sin. In her mind, it was something she and Sam 'just had to work out'.

Jerk.

Sam left her. So did the lead singer.

Even when we are being 'spiritual', we can be jerks. I still cringe when I think of the time I publicly interrupted a pastor whose prayer bugged me. There we were, a roomful of pastors, on our knees, praying with passion and energy for our hometown city of Chicago.

The prayer time was free-form: pastors prayed for various needs as we saw fit. One colleague and pastor was doing just that, when I rudely interrupted him. I didn't like his prayer. Okay, maybe he went on way too long praying over a topic that I wasn't very happy about – a prayer I couldn't really say 'amen' to. Still, he prayed in a legitimate way for a legitimate need.

That didn't stop me.

The more he prayed, the more my Inner Jerk got riled up. My eyes watched and my ears listened as my Inner Mess conscripted my mouth into the service of my Inner Jerk. I heard my mouth say, 'All right! That's ENOUGH.' Right in the middle of his prayer.

Every head jerked to attention.

In case you don't know, interrupting a fellow pastor in a public prayer meeting is not something we pastors normally do. But my Inner Jerk was driving the bus. I just sat in the passenger's seat and watched.

My eyes saw him look up at me with a 'deer in the headlights' look.

My conscience smacked me in the head, trying to regain control of my vocal apparatus. It lost. My Inner Mess, anticipating my spasms of conscience, has *shielded* its high-speed connection to my mouth.

My mouth continued: 'Can we please move on to something else?'

'Uhh... wow... I'm sorry... I didn't mean to offend,' he said.

'That's all right. Let's just move on.'

The jerk in me salutes the jerk in you. When your Inner Jerk slithers forth, your family and friends – and even your pastors – run for cover. Let's see what makes the Inner Jerk such a... uhhh... jerk.

Past Problems

> *And you, fathers, do not provoke your children to wrath,*
> *but bring them up in the training and admonition of the*
> *Lord.*
>
> (Ephesians 6:4)

Many Inner Mess patterns stem from a parent who 'provoked us to wrath'. Through either commission or omission, our mom or dad wounded us. Your Inner Mess buzzes around those wounds like flies around rotting meat.

Research from the National Fatherhood Initiative[1] reveals how kids react when our parents – especially our dads – don't do their job. I'm not giving you these statistics to condemn single mothers or to make you feel bad if you've failed your kids. I just want to highlight some chapters in *your* story that probably sent your Inner Mess over the edge – especially your Inner Jerk. These would be the chapters in which Daddy let you down big time. Consider the numbers.

A study of nearly 14,000 women in prison showed that more than half grew up without their father. Forty-two per cent grew up in a single-mother household and sixteen per cent lived with neither parent.[2] A study of more than 100 juvenile offenders indicated that family structure significantly predicts delinquency.[3] There is far greater drug use among children who do not live with their mother and father.[4]

I include this data only to invite you to connect some dots between your Inner Jerk and the trauma of your past.

'A major study of child abuse in dozens of countries found that children from single-parent families are more likely to be victims of physical and sexual abuse than children who live with both of their biological parents. Compared to other kids who were living with both parents, children in single, fatherless homes faced:

• a 77 per cent greater risk of being physically abused
• an 87 per cent greater risk of being harmed by physical neglect
• a 165 per cent greater risk of experiencing notable physical neglect
• a 74 per cent greater risk of suffering from emotional neglect
• an 80 per cent greater risk of suffering serious injury as a result of abuse
• overall, a 120 per cent greater risk of being endangered by some type of child abuse.'[5]

Kids naturally look to parents, especially to fathers, for protection from harm. When Dad lets you down, you react with bitterness, sowing the seeds of your Inner Jerk. That bitterness, the Bible teaches, causes trouble and damages our relationships (Hebrews 12:15).

Children living in a two-parent household with a poor relationship with their father are 68 per cent more likely to smoke, drink, or use drugs compared to teens in two-parent households. Being raised by a single mother raises the risk of teen pregnancy, marrying with less than a high-school degree, and forming a marriage in which both partners have less than a high-school degree.[6] What's going on?

These are behaviors of a child crying out for a father's attention.

Is this to say, 'Shame on you, single parent!'? Not at all. Many single parents deserve awards for the heroic task they undertake. I'm not condemning you or anybody else. I'm writing to bring you face to face with forces that shaped, and still shape, *your* life.

And one of those main forces is your father. Whenever a dad is absent, distracted, addicted, self-absorbed, abusive, legalistic, disapproving, a workaholic, or a churchaholic, he wounds his child's spirit. This, in turn, powerfully triggers your Inner Mess to trash your outer world.

Our problem is that either we fail to realize anything is wrong, or we fail to connect the dots between our past wound – and its unresolved anger – and our present problems. Wherever cluelessness reigns, the Inner Mess steps in.

Jesus taught, 'And why do you look at the speck in your brother's eye, but do not consider the plank in your own eye? Or how can you say to your brother, "Let me remove the speck from your eye"; and look, a plank is in your own eye? Hypocrite! First remove the plank from your own eye, and then you will see clearly to remove the speck from your brother's eye' (Matthew 7:3–5).

Let's associate that passenger on your bus who revels in 'the speck in your brother's or sister's eye' with your Inner Jerk. Mean, harsh, unkind, critical, fault-finding, superior and obnoxious. This is the part of you that makes your kids cautious and makes your spouse walk on eggshells. It also makes your pastor worry about your next e-mail.

What is your Inner Jerk's main problem?

Jesus says your Inner Jerk suffers from *Plank in the eye syndrome*. Ouch! That has to hurt, don't you think? A plank in the eye, by anybody's definition, is a *wound*. But instead of dealing with the real wound, and the real 'wounder,' your Inner Jerk takes it out on others. So you take it as your 'Christian' mission to point out the minutest speck in everybody else's eye, all the while ignoring the two-by-four in yours.

Every time your Inner Jerk commandeers the bus you re-enact some unfinished drama from your past.

Your mouth shouts at your children, but your Inner Jerk is really shouting at your lousy father.

You lash out at your husband, but your heart lashes out at your drunken father.

You kick the dog, while your soul wishes you could kick your dad.

You raise the shields against intimacy, but you're really raising the shields against reliving the pain that your father failed to prevent.

When the drama is over, you feel terrible. You realize what a jerk you've been. But you can't seem to muster the soul-strength to make things right. And you certainly haven't figured out how to change.

So which drama did I re-enact when I censored my friend's prayer?

It took me a while to figure it out. But that pastoral prayer meeting was partly my baby. I helped initiate it. My Inner Mess linked the success of the prayer meeting with my own value and worth as a spiritual leader. My status among my peers depended on it.

The aliens in my head shrieked something like this: *He's wrecking the prayer meeting! If people keep praying like that, attendance will shrink. If attendance shrinks, you won't be famous! You won't be important! You won't be glorious! Stop him! Stop him! Stop him! STOP HIM! DO SOMETHING!*

Consider me praise-deprived, a cardinal symptom of the father-wound.

My Inner Jerk galloped to the rescue. I shut my colleague up so that he wouldn't spoil my glory. That strategy backfired.

Plank-in-the-eye syndrome has an annoying habit of playing invisible when you try to find it. Our biggest faults are invisible to ourselves; we don't see them by looking directly at them. Instead we see them by the results: a very active Inner Jerk who trashes a lot of the good in your life and unleashes your frustrations on your colleague, sister, brother, girlfriend, boyfriend, friends, husband, wife, or kids. Or strangers. Or your dog.

Worst of all, your Inner Mess uses your father-wound as a perfect excuse to redefine God – almost always in the image of your failed father. MEMO TO INNER MESS: My Heavenly Father is infinitely better than my earthly father.

The father-wound energizes the Jerk in you. If you don't see how, I can practically guarantee that you suffer from plank-in-the-eye syndrome.

Other Wounds

There are other wounds beside the father-wound. Here are some common wounds that scar the soul. Underline the ones that resonate with you. If you're just plain numb to most of it, then underline the ones that any objective observer would say were part of your life. Really, underline them. Unless this is a borrowed book; in that case, just make a list.

Abandonment, physical abuse, sexual abuse, emotional abuse, feelings of being lost, never knowing your dad, never knowing your mom, constant belittling, emotionally distant parents, growing up in a hyper-sexualized home, parents who were impossible to please, hyper-religious parents, growing up in legalism, never feeling approval, loss of a sibling, violence, alcoholic or drug-addicted parent/s, growing up ignored, criticized, or in somebody else's shadow.

As often as you re-enact the unfinished dramas of your past, as long as you take vengeance on yourself or others, you're like a rag doll in the mouth of a Rottweiler: shaken to shreds by your Inner Mess.

It doesn't have to be that way. Jesus tells you to remove the plank from your own eye. So it can be done.

But you have to see it to remove it. That's the tricky part.

What Do You Condemn?

During my freshman year at a Christian college, a professor publicly criticized a children's ministry that I was involved in. He didn't know I had championed that ministry most of my life. My loyalty overcame my fear of confronting a professor. I made an appointment and we met. I blurted out that a lot of kids were helped by that ministry and I knew for a fact that some of my fellow students had considered helping out until he unleashed his criticisms and that was wrong and why did he do that?

I, a no-account freshman, rebuked a professor and chairman of the department at a major Christian college.

Maybe I have the spiritual gift of rebuking.

To his credit the professor took it well and quickly apologized to me. In the next class session, he modified his critique to praise the children's ministry itself while criticizing only some specific aspects of it.

But something he said during our meeting stuck with me: 'We criticize in others the things we like least about ourselves.' It resonated with me. It resonates with Scripture too:

> *'You, therefore, have no excuse, you who pass judgment on someone else, for at whatever point you judge the other, you are condemning yourself, because you who pass judgment do the same things' (Romans 2:1, NIV).*

Your Inner Jerk condemns others for doing the same things you do.

Come on, admit it: don't your kids aggravate you most when they resemble you most? When their stupidity reflects your stupidity?

I condemned a pastor for hijacking a prayer meeting and turning it to his agenda. What I didn't understand back then was that I had done the same thing. I had – to some degree – defined the prayer meeting as something other than entirely a prayer meeting. It was also a personal promotion for my spiritual gigantic-ness in our pastoral community. *That prayer meeting's mine! I hijacked it first! Give it back to me!*

What do you criticize? What do you condemn with disproportionate energy? What flaws do you see in others? What makes you ticked off and crabby? These are flashing neon signs pointing at your Inner Jerk. Pay attention. The speck in your sister or brother's eye *is* the plank in your eye.

What Do You Repeat?

If two or more people tell you you're a jerk (crabby, mean, harsh, judgmental, legalistic or abusive), believe them. Thank them. Don't argue with them. And put 'jerkiness' on the list of Inner Mess problems you need to tackle.

Your Inner Mess operates in patterns. You rarely violate a boundary once; you violate it repeatedly. We are all serial sinners.

Ancient biblical law required two witnesses to convict of a crime (Deuteronomy 19:15). Two eyewitnesses. Or one eyewitness plus physical evidence. Or physical evidence plus a confession. Or two single eyewitnesses to you repeating the same crime twice.

So if one eyewitness testifies that I stole a candy bar last Friday that's not enough to convict. But if a second eyewitness testifies that I stole a candy bar on Saturday too, I'm guilty as charged.

This is very smart policy. Your Inner Mess behaviors run in patterns. Once you unleash your Inner Jerk, it usually stays unleashed and terrorizes the neighborhood. This explains criminal recidivism. It also explains why your sister married a jerk and then divorced him only to marry another jerk. Her Inner Mess runs in patterns.

It also explains why your Inner Jerk can wreak such havoc in your outer world. In the world of the Inner Mess, once is not enough. Your flesh is not content merely to cause a wound; your flesh has to rub it raw.

That's why you should take it to heart whenever multiple friends, family or colleagues muster the courage to point out your unkindness. Or sever relationships with you. Or beg you to change.

You have a plank stuck in your eye and can't see it. All you can see is the little speck, the imperfection, in the other person. You obsess over it. In fact, most of the time, it was you who put the speck there in the first place.

You can trace your present conflicts to your past wounds. Thank you, Inner Mess.

Until you heal the wounds through grace, you'll keep meeting the same conflicts over and over again. It won't help to change schools, find a new job, move to a new city, or trade in your old spouse for a new one. You can't run from you.

As soon as you throw a suitcase on the bed to pack your bags for greener pastures, what do you think your Inner Mess does? It's on the other side of the bed packing as fast as you are. 'Oh no! Don't you think you're going anywhere without me. You can't leave me. I'll show you.'

As long as you expect other people to change, and are unwilling to change yourself, you are exactly the person Jesus talks about in Matthew 7:3–5. You've been taking out your unacknowledged pain on others.

And that is the hulking force behind so many Inner Mess woes. So how do we break the cycle of past wounds that cause and re-cause present problems?

Rewrite the Scripts

When the jerks in your life inflicted their cruelty on impressionable little you, you took it in. You internalized their cruelty. Their unkind words and behaviours transmogrified into mental and emotional scripts. These scripts play in (and on) your mind. Here are some sample scripts:

- You're stupid.
- You'll never amount to anything.
- You can't do anything right.
- Nobody could ever love you.
- If you don't listen, I won't love you.
- I hate you.
- I wish you'd never been born.
- Wipe that stupid smile off your face.
- I'll give you something to cry about.
- Failure!

Whenever you feel threatened, your flesh presses 'PLAY' on one of your scripts. You relive your father-wound. You feel the pain of the past. And you re-enact the unfinished drama.

You don't really live. You cope.

I know this seems heavy and maybe even hopeless, but hang in there and keep reading. Jesus does not just diagnose our problems – he is the Great Physician. He can bring healing into this mess. We will learn how in the second half of this book.

We're going to write some new scripts. It might not be easy to install them onto your spiritual hard drive, but you can do it. By God's power, you can displace the old Inner Mess scripts with new scripts written on your heart by God's Spirit.

And if anyone ever interrupts you during the middle of a public prayer, show a little mercy. I couldn't help myself.

Taking Out the Trash

How have you recently unleashed your Inner Jerk? How did you feel afterwards? How do you think the other person felt?

Describe the last time you were on the receiving end of somebody else's Inner Jerk. How did you feel afterwards? How do you think the other person felt?

Though you may dearly love and appreciate your dad, he was not perfect. How does your father-wound affect your life and relationships?

How has your father-wound distorted your view of God? What negative opinions of God do you hold that you can trace to your earthly father's failings? Make a list and visit www.innermess.com for a selection of Scripture passages that can help rehabilitate your view of God.

Have you ever mistakenly hoped that a change in your outer world would change your inner spirit? What kind of external changes have you tried (for example, changing jobs, spouses, facial appearance, etc)?

What is meant by the 'carnal mind' in Romans 8:7: 'Because the carnal mind *is* enmity against God; for it is not subject to the law of God, nor indeed can be'?

Prayer: For the humility to meet your Inner Jerk.

Chapter 5
Your Inner Dummy

'A hurricane of afflictions may beat about you, yet you shall be a blessed man, for all the elements of blessedness are within your own heart. God has given them to you, and the devil himself cannot take them away.'

Charles H. Spurgeon, 1876[1]

Scott debated before opening the door. Once he started rolling, regulations didn't require him to stop, even if someone pounded on the door. The rainy day and his compassion got the better of him. Scott braked and opened the door. He was sure he'd regret it.

He didn't know how right he was.

She climbed on board.

High heels clicked up two steps to the fare box. The passengers smelled her cheap perfume before they saw her. Scott noticed the vacant look in her prematurely aged eyes. She looked used up. Life had not been kind to her. Men had not been kind to her.

'Hi, sweetie,' she said as she deposited her token.

Scott hated it when she called him that. He just nodded. The bus lurched forward.

Everything about her screamed 'too much'. Too much perfume. Too much make-up. Too much cleavage. Too much body squeezed into not enough clothing. Scott once described her to his wife: 'She doesn't exactly walk; she prowls.'

Her eyes scanned the bus. The felon looked her up and

down and back up. He licked his lips without realizing and shifted position.

Scott noticed the tract lady stiffen her back. For the first time that day, he felt amused. The tract lady was about to blow a blood vessel. Clearly, she couldn't decide who needed her ministrations more – the felon or the hooker. She reached out a hand and touched the hooker's arm as she swept by.

'I'd like to talk with you,' she said.

The hooker looked down and rolled her eyes. She spoke in a loud whisper. 'Not now, honey. I'm working.' She shook off the tract lady's hand and reached the seat next to the well-dressed man reading the newspaper.

Jason closed his eyes. Scott watched with interest. He'd never seen Jason look unnerved before today.

Not today of all days. Jason felt her slide into the seat next to him. He could smell past her perfume all the way to her body. He felt her leg press against his. He pulled away.

'So how's she treating you?'

'Pardon?'

'The stock market. I'm just asking how she's treating you. You look like a trader. You trade, don't you? I hear it's been nothing but up and down.' She smiled thick, red lips at him.

Jason stammered, 'W-well, uhh. I was uhhh…'

He was mercifully interrupted by the tract lady. She'd gotten up and was standing over the hooker. 'I really think we need to talk. I have something that could help you. The Lord has a message for you.'

'Listen, lady, there ain't nothin' you could say that my daddy didn't tell me a thousand times when he wasn't messin' with me. I told you, not today.'

'One day, you'll be sorry and it will be too late. At least read this.' Her tract fluttered down and settled in the hooker's cleavage. The tract lady snorted and stomped to her seat. The hooker laughed. She flipped the tract to the floor and let her hand linger where the tract had been.

'Now, where were we?' She fixed her eyes on Jason.

His eyes opened wide. But he wasn't looking at the hooker sitting next to him...

* * *

With the Lord's authority I say this: Live no longer as the ungodly do, for they are hopelessly confused.

(Ephesians 4:17, NLT)

'Swing the bat, Bill! Swing the stupid bat!'
'Strike two!'
Hey, that was outside!
'Swing the bat! Just swing it.'
I stood motionless.
'Ball three!'
Yes!

I could actually hit and field well. In the playground. With my friends. But come game time, I choked. As I recall, my childhood logic concluded that if I didn't swing, I couldn't miss. I could conceivably walk. Yes, I could get called out on strikes, but, for that, I could blame the umpire.

What freaked me out was swinging and *missing*. I chose to play the odds and hope for walks. Walks are not unusual in Little League. I made getting them my highest ambition.

In practice I could hit as well as anybody else. But in games, when it counted, I just stood there. Tense. Immobilized. Fearing failure. During an entire Little League baseball season at Oriole Park in Chicago, I think I swung the bat four times. Remarkably, I chalked up two hits. I also chalked up a massive number of walks and strikeouts for which I either thanked or blamed the umpire.

When it was my turn to bat, I stood frozen in place. Neither feet nor bat nor head nor mouth moved. I just stood there, watching pitches go by, and hoping that my brother or dad wasn't watching.

71

We once came across a fawn during a hike with our friends and their kids. No bigger than a small dog, it lay motionless in the tall grass, curled into a ball. Its brown color and light spots camouflaged it well. My friends' kids asked if it were dead and why it didn't run away. We explained that God taught the fawn to freeze when it sensed danger.

A part of every human soul has learned the same lesson.

Blanking Out

We'll use the term 'blanking out' for those moments when your Inner Mess locks down your brain in the panic room of your soul. It's like 'spacing out', but comes more from your Inner Mess than from your general flakiness. When you blank out, you can't think or speak or hear or see very well. You stop feeling. You go to your 'happy place'. You distance yourself from the reality of the moment, doing or saying what, to any rational observer, doesn't make sense. You choke.

Blanking out is any pattern your Inner Mess creates to avoid dealing with your deepest issues, feeling your deepest feelings, or pursuing your deepest desires.

The underlying emotion of blanking out is fear. Fear of rejection, death, abandonment, failure, exposure, aloneness, or pain. These are valid fears and there are better ways to handle them. Blanking out is your flesh's way.

The tragedy is that the longer you blank out, the more your irretrievable and precious *life* passes you by. There are several varieties of blanking out

Deaf and Blind. High anxiety constricts your ability to hear and see. Your angry wife speaks and your ears hear an onslaught of words, but nothing registers with your mind. Later she'll be even angrier because she thought she had already told you the stuff you didn't hear.

How many times have you lost your car keys before an important interview or a big date? You tear the house apart only to find your keys hiding in plain sight on the counter where you'd already looked a half-dozen times. Your optical apparatus saw your keys, but your Inner Dummy – operating in panic mode – intercepted the neural transmission and made you go as good as blind *just to your keys*.

An activated Inner Mess holds the keys to your body and perceptions. When threatened, you stop noticing what's around you. A colleague says 'hello' to you, but you don't hear her because you are blanking out. She thinks you're rude. You aren't, though. You're just freaked out, even if it doesn't show.

Dumb. To prepare for my first and only trip to Italy, I studied Italian with my friend, Silvia. A native of Florence, Silvia equipped me to ask for water, find a bathroom, greet her family, and buy a basic meal. I studied hard and was ready. When we got off the train in Florence, Silvia's lovely mother greeted me warmly in the most melodic and elementary Italian – in phrases her daughter promised her I'd understand. Spoken slowly as to a six-year old.

It was performance time. Time to show how much I'd learned. Time to step up to the plate.

I do not have a good track record at this.

She had me at 'Ciao'. After that, my mind went blank and all that registered was a torrent of gibberish. All I could say was, 'Silviaaa! Help!'

My Inner Dummy drove the bus right off a mental cliff. Blanking out makes you lose your mind, stop thinking, stumble over words, or become forgetful. When you blank out, you become absent-minded, scatterbrained, mentally paralyzed, and forgetful of appointments, names, times, and anniversaries.

Why do you think you forget a new name within seconds of hearing it? Your Inner Mess is much too busy dealing with a very present fear to devote any resources whatsoever to any other person.

What was your name again?

Distant. As an aspiring young pastor it was my delight to

visit a mega-church led by a pastor who sometimes mentored me. My crowning disappointment came during a conversation with him between worship services at his church. As long as he focused on our conversation, I felt like the king of the world. But his eyes kept wandering to more important people in the lobby. Mentally, he wasn't with me. He was chatting with me, but wasn't all there. He might as well have been a million miles away.

Sometimes the fear of failure motivates constant surveillance so that we can deploy our scarce resources – in this case, time and energy – to the efforts most likely to prop up our fragile ego. He distanced himself, not because I was unworthy, but because he was insecure.

Detached. The longer your Inner Mess dominates you, the more calloused your emotions become. Yes, you have a sensitive core, but – if your Inner Mess has its way – nobody touches it. The Bible talks about having a hardened heart (Ephesians 4:17–19). A calloused heart. This doesn't make you a *bad* person. It makes you a *scared* person who has consigned the management of your fear to the Inner Mess. So you detach yourself from anything even remotely scary, especially from intimacy and its risks. Your Inner Dummy coats your soul as DuPont coats non-stick pans. You shed pain as a duck sheds water.

Your spouse, kids, family and friends desperately want to engage the emotional side of you. Ideally, you can express your emotions in ways that are straight and clean. But when you can't, any form of emotion will do. Even toxic ones.

Rather than get all messy and emotional, it's much easier to just shut down your feelings. Your Inner Dummy is only too glad to cooperate.

The Bible identifies flesh-dominated people as those whose minds are darkened and who *have lost all sensitivity and care* (Ephesians 4:18,19). Thanks, flesh. What would I do without you?

Denial. Do you remember sixth grade, that day when

your math teacher turned her back, and the whole class let fly a fusillade of spitballs aimed at the chalkboard? Do you remember how your teacher whirled around fast enough to give a snake whiplash, only to see the entire class sitting like perfect little ladies and gentlemen? Hands folded on the desk? Angelic expressions? 'Who, *me*?' written across every brow? Remember how your teacher ran out of the classroom sobbing?

Do you remember? No? Oh. Never mind.

So sorry, Ms. Robinson.

What do you think happens when you stomp your way to the back of your bus, demanding to know *Who did that?* Every Inner Mess character plays Shirley Temple. An innocent angel. 'Who, *me*? There is no problem, and if there were a problem, I didn't do it.'

Ever since Adam and Eve covered themselves with fig leaves, our flesh has been covering itself in denial.

Dead. Your Inner Dummy wants you dead. Not necessarily physically dead, though that might be part of it. (If it is, I urge you to get professional help immediately.) But emotionally dead. Numb. Dumb. Feeling no pain.

Paul identifies this as being 'alienated from the life of God' (Ephesians 4:18). Instead of pursuing the dreams that electrify your spirit, your flesh makes you 'settle'. You settle for a boring, bland, vanilla, safe excuse for a life.

All because real life scares you. And a real relationship with a real man or woman scares you too. And the real risk you run of failure scares you.

So you stand, paralyzed, while opportunities keep flying by. And you never swing the bat.

One day, the opportunities will stop.

Blanking-Out Behaviors

Let's get really specific about the behaviors of a blanked-out soul. Let me say that some of these behaviors can have underlying medical causes, and you should use God's gift of the medical profession. See a doctor. Stay on your medications.

Other times, however, these behaviors emanate from the garbage dump in your soul. Here's a partial list:

- Drug addiction, to deaden the pain of an empty life.
- Alcohol addiction, including being a weekend drunk.
- Workaholism, a way of avoiding attachment and intimacy.
- Television or Internet addiction. Come in, sit down, turn on the technology, feel nothing for five hours, lose your life, and go emotionally dead. Those who love you most know when your real-life relationships, obligations or dreams suffer because of technology. Websites such as *Second Life* and *World of Warcraft* create imaginary worlds for millions of people. One young man in my church told me he sat down to play *Warcraft* for a little while, and when he looked up, eight hours had passed. Millions of real dollars are spent every day on *Second Life*. I know that countless people use these sites as harmless pastimes. But for many more they are ways of killing time while avoiding life. Why? Because the flesh employs ingenious strategies to avoid the risks of a real life.
- Unusual absentmindedness, forgetfulness, or scatterbrained behavior. For some of us, that's just part of our temperament. But many times our unacknowledged fears are showing.
- Obsessive hobbies or interests. It could be anything: gardening, learning a language, fishing, woodworking, sewing, knitting, cleaning, martial arts. These are all healthy aspects of a balanced life, until they become an excuse to stay away from intimacy.
- Isolation. Keeping busy alone; turning into a hermit.

- Physical paralysis. There's a reason we say that in a big situation, someone 'choked.' That's why sports such as golf, baseball and basketball are such mental sports. Next time you slice your tee shot, blame your Inner Dummy.
- Pornography. Just another way your Inner Mess avoids the vulnerability that comes with love.
- Inhibited sexual desire. Call it fear of intimacy, call it 'I'm too tired.' It's still not God's plan for married couples, and there is help for you, if you're courageous enough to take it.
- Uncommitted sex or impersonal sex. Let's include one-night stands here. Let's call this fear of intimacy, too. Impersonal, uncommitted sex is a frantic grasping after *intensity*, because the rest of your life is so emotionally dead. After a while, even your uncommitted sex loses intensity. That's why Somebody far wiser and more loving than us instructs us to reserve sex for the committed, personal relationship called marriage.

The High Price of Blanking Out

Continual blanking out comes with a high price tag.

Boredom. You lead a boring, safe, bland, vanilla life. Every day is the same as every other day.

Broken and shallow relationships, because anybody with even half a life won't put up with your constant blanking out.

Desperation. People who blank out eventually become so past feeling that they need increasingly intense experiences to feel anything at all. More nicotine, more sex, more porn, more food, more money, more women/men, more danger, more risk, more power, more deviancy. The Bible uses the word 'greed' to describe this frantic grasping after happiness (Ephesians 4:19). One translation calls it 'a continual lust for more' (Ephesians 4:19, NIV).

No life. Hence the phrase, 'Get a life.'

Hence this book on how to keep your Inner Mess from trashing your outer world. *How,* you ask?

The secret is simple but tough.

I became a hero to my team at the last at-bat of my Little League career. The other team called a 'pansy shift'. That means the pitcher waved in the outfielders because he knew I wouldn't swing. The outfielders stood at the edge of the dirt infield. The infielders practically took off their mitts and sat down.

I felt embarrassed. This was the first time a team called a pansy shift on me. Something in me rose to the occasion. Call it indignation. Call it anger. Call it determination.

The pitcher took the mound. He smacked the ball into his glove a few times. He reared back and threw.

I closed my eyes.

I swung the bat.

I heard the satisfying crack of a baseball rocketing off a wooden bat. I opened my eyes in time to see the stunned looks of the other team. I heard the cheers of my fellow Oriole Park Twins. I watched with satisfaction as the ball sailed over the left fielder's head and bounced down the third-base line. He turned and chased it.

I ran as fast as my ten-year-old legs could carry me.

I learned a secret that day.

I can't get a hit if I don't swing the bat.

And you can't feel really alive unless you take one hundred per cent of the responsibility to move *into* your fears constantly. You have to do the thing that scares you most. Swing the bat. Risk the failure. Take the leap.

I'd like to say I rounded the bases for a home run. I didn't. But I'll settle for a triple any day.

Decades later, I can remember that day. I can taste that day. I was alive. Heroic. I took a risk and survived. For that golden afternoon I basked in the feeling of being all alive.

All the stuff that my Inner Mess fears, all the stuff that

makes me blank out – that's where my life is. I just have to make contact.

Taking Out the Trash

....

Tell about a time when you 'choked' – when you were paralyzed by fear or indecision. What were you really afraid of?

Your Inner Mess, when threatened, blanks you out by making you deaf, blind, dumb, distant, detached, and dead. Have you seen any of these fear reactions in yourself or family lately?

Review the list of blanking-out *behaviors* from this chapter. Which ones do you struggle with? What do you think motivates these behaviors?

Can you spot some of your routine activities that suck the life out of you? Choices that make you emotionally and spiritually numb? Or that make your friends and family worry you're spending too much time on them?

How does 2 Timothy 1:7 apply to blanking out: 'For God has not given us a spirit of fear, but of power and of love and of a sound mind'?

Read 2 Kings 7:3–11. What was the four men's status? What were their options? Which one did they pick? How might they have felt? What did moving into their fears gain them?

Prayer: For God's spirit of power, love, and a sound mind to characterize your inner life.

Chapter 6
Your Inner Brat

'See that… you content not yourselves with seeming to do good in outward acts, when you are bad yourselves, and strangers to the great internal duties. The first and great work of a Christian is about his heart.'

Richard Baxter, 1615–91

'What's the matter, honey?' The hooker followed Jason's eyes to the front of the bus. She saw an attractive woman insert money into the fare box. She was slender with wet blonde hair pulled back in a ponytail. An expensive-looking, water-resistant jogging suit shed large droplets onto white running shoes. Her chest rose and fell with the heavy breathing of someone who'd been running hard.

The woman scanned the bus, looking for someone. She found Jason. Jason swallowed hard and opened his mouth. The woman's eyes then moved to the hooker next to him. Her head tilted to the side as she looked back at Jason.

'Why don't I just go visit with somebody else?' The hooker mobilized her ample body up and out of her seat. She moved to the last row and sat next to a sleeping twenty-something man in a crooked baseball cap who was trying to grow a beard.

Scott noticed the dripping woman's body tense up. He let his bus roll forward to the yellow cab ahead and stopped. In his mirror he could see Jason start to rise, but then sink back into his seat as the woman's hand motioned him down.

With her other hand she held up what looked like a tube of lipstick. Scott watched as Jason's face registered confusion, then recognition, then the wretchedness of a man about to vomit. Jason dropped his head. His ears burned red. His shoulders drooped. He sank lower in his seat with each step that the pony-tailed woman took toward him.

No one could foresee that the woman wouldn't reach Jason unscathed.

* * *

Brats Making Headlines

From Court TV News: A sex offender wanted in Florida fled into the frigid woods of wintry New England. Mr. Harvey Bainton, 48, allegedly spent three nights on the lam, trudging through knee-deep snow. He was arrested on February 11. Doctors amputated three toes on his left foot because of frostbite. Mr. Bainton promptly threatened to sue. From his hospital bed the fugitive charged, 'If [the detective] had done his job properly, I wouldn't be in here now.'[1]

From the State of Michigan, Court of Appeals, Case No. 264119: A woman sued Coca Cola and her local grocery store when a can of soda sprayed her face and burned her eyes. The alleged victim retrieved a can of Diet Coke from her garage, opened it, and was shocked when the can spewed its moderately acidic contents into her face and (apparently wide-open) eyes. She sued because the can does not warn consumers that its 'contents may exit the can at high velocity' and cause injury.[2]

If it weren't for our Inner Brats, how would lawyers survive?

One of the most infamous cases of brat behavior in professional basketball came courtesy of the Chicago Bulls. In the year that Michael Jordan retired, Scottie Pippen raised his game to a new level. He led the team to almost as many wins as Jordan had the season before. In the '93–'94 playoffs, Scottie unleashed his Inner Brat before 18,676 roaring Chicago fans and millions of stunned – and disgusted – TV viewers.

On 13 May, 1994, with 1.8 seconds left in the third playoff game against the despised New York Knicks, Coach Phil Jackson called for Pippen's teammate, Tony Kukoç, to take the final shot. Pippen would inbound the ball to Kukoç who would shoot. That play had already won two games in the final seconds.

Pippen was angry. He had, at long last, emerged from Jordan's shadow to lead the team. This shot belonged to him. He argued with Jackson in the huddle. Jackson wouldn't budge. Pippen threw a tantrum. He swore and sat down.

When the timeout ended, only four Bulls stepped onto the court. Teammates begged Pippen to get in the game. The officials were about to start play. Jackson had to call another timeout. He told Pippen to get into the game.

Pippen wouldn't budge.

This story might be apocryphal, but my dad swears that he once dumped a spoonful of peas into my seven-year-old mouth and barked at me, 'You'll sit there till you eat it.'

Three hours later, he told me to spit it out and go to bed.

Scottie, I'm with you, man.

Kukoç scored the game-winning basket. Scottie Pippen watched from the bench.

When my sixth-grade substitute teacher ordered me into the hallway, I knew I'd crossed a line. Even though she seemed a hundred years old, she wasn't too old to put the fear of God into me. She got me into the hallway, leaned close to my eleven-year-old face and whispered low, so no one else could hear: 'I wish I could slap your face.'

I bet that's how Jackson felt about Pippen that day.

Our Four Needs

Your Inner Brat pouts, throws tantrums, and trashes your outer world over the unfinished business of early childhood needs. You introduced yourself to the world with a wail of neediness. With bad nurturing, the wail never goes away; it just sounds deeper when your voice changes.

Even worse, it stomps to the front of the bus and spoils the party for everyone. It's time to coax this sullen, dour, demanding part of your flesh out of hiding.

Your Inner Brat mounts guard over four basic needs:

• Notice me!
• Satisfy me!
• Accept me!
• Help me!

These are valid needs. If they're not met, you die. God equipped even the tiniest infant with a potent arsenal to reward caregivers who meet these needs and to punish caregivers who don't.

Long after we leave behind the diapers and pacifiers, these needs remain.

God made us this way so he could hardwire our brains with his overarching policy for the human race: Grace. The only reason we've survived this long is because of other people's sacrifices. No one is self-made. No one can boast. We all have needs.

That includes your spouse. And your parents, roommate, boss, employees, kids and friends. Ditto for your crabby neighbor and successful uncle. Even Scottie Pippen. Bill Gates. Eminem. David Beckham and Michael Jordan. Maroon 5 and the Rolling Stones. Each one has a little voice squeaking: Notice me, satisfy me, accept me, help me.

Don't get me wrong; these needs are valid. I'd even call them healthy.

But once your Inner Mess gets involved, everything turns ugly. Your Inner Mess gnaws on your basic needs like Gollum on a raw fish.

James declared, 'You have not because you ask not'

(James 4:2). That verse makes many readers think of prayer. But James didn't originally write this verse about prayer. He wrote it about *relationships* and about getting our needs met in the context of relationships. Especially messy ones:

> *Where do wars and fights come from among you? Do they not come from your desires for pleasure that war in your members? You lust and do not have. You murder and covet and cannot obtain. You fight and war. Yet you do not have because you do not ask. You ask and do not receive, because you ask amiss, that you may spend it on your pleasures (James 4:1–3).*

The healthy way – the *holy* way – to get your needs met is to ask. Straight-up, honest, humble asking in the context of open, transparent relationships. But that is exactly where it gets dicey. The only way your flesh knows how to *ask* is by fighting, whining, conniving, hinting, pouting, and sniveling like a spoiled, sugar-overdosed brat. Here's what that might look like.

Your Inner Brat and Your Four Needs

Notice Me!

As an infant you possessed an ear-piercing method of getting noticed. When my kids were little, I could hear their cries three rooms away with a jet flying overhead and a king-sized pillow crammed over my ears. Their cries lifted me to DEFCON 1. My wife and I *noticed* them. We couldn't *not* notice them. Even to this day their cries jolt us with adrenaline.

But what if your parents were too wasted, drunk, self-absorbed or busy to notice you? What does a kid have to do to get some attention around here?

How about getting so many body piercings that we could hook you to a hose and water the lawn?

Or how about going on a crime spree? Or letting your

jeans ride lower than your rear end? Or refusing to play when the coach sends you in?

BRATTY PIPPEN: I want the game-winning shot. I want the glory. Me. Me. Me. That shot's mine! After all I've done for this team. I want the screaming adoration of thousands and thousands of adoring, worshipping fans. I…
NOBLE PIPPEN: Hey, but we're a team. It's the playoffs. There's no 'I' in…
BRATTY PIPPEN: All my life I've fought to get noticed. Michael is gone – finally. Now it's my turn to shine.
INNER LAWYER PIPPEN: Coach Jackson is robbing me!
NOBLE PIPPEN: He's not robbing you! He's giving you a victory. You'll get noticed as the guy who put the team first. The fans will love you.
INNER LAWYER PIPPEN: Don't talk to my client. Scottie, you don't have to answer that.
BRATTY PIPPEN: That's it! If I don't shoot, I don't play.

You have two options for getting noticed: the direct way and the indirect way. The indirect way is the way of your Inner Mess. It is also the way that generates headlines.

The direct way might sound like this: 'Honey, did you notice that I mowed the lawn?' Or, 'What do you think of my new hairstyle?'

Its no good saying, 'He should have noticed without my having to ask.' 'You have not because you ask not,' remember? God puts the burden of *asking* on you. Don't try to turn it into someone else's burden to *notice*. Unless, of course, you want to be high-maintenance *all* your life.

But what if you don't want to ask directly? What if you're too vain, proud or shy? What if it's not *manly* to ask someone to notice you?

This is the law of the Inner Mess: your soul hands-off unexpressed needs to your Inner Mess as a quarterback hands-off to his running back. Your 'notice me' need then becomes indirect, doubles in strength and turns toxic. Here are some indirect ways in which people get noticed without directly asking:

- Workaholism
- Addictive behaviors
- Acting up
- Self-destructive tendencies (anorexia, bulimia, cutting, hair-pulling, any disorder that ends with -mania)
- Bullying
- Perfectionism: too neat, good, clean, smart, organized or holy
- Overconsciousness of looks, physique, style, or make-up
- Dress, hair or speech styles way out of the cultural norm
- Out of the cultural norm piercings and tattoos
- Bragging – I'm better than you!
- Whining, complaining – 'You never notice my _____!'
- Frequent comparisons with others
- Dominating conversations.

You need to be noticed. We all do. When your Inner Brat takes over that need, its motto is 'Bad strokes are better than no strokes.'

Satisfy Me!

One of the dumbest pieces of advice I've ever received came from friends while dining at our favorite all-you-can-eat buffet: 'Eat really fast so your stomach doesn't have time to signal your brain that it's full.' When I first heard said dumb advice, I felt enlightened, like an initiate into an inner circle of esoteric knowledge.

Minutes later – while repressing the urge to retch, loosening my belt, unsnapping my jeans, leaning back in my chair, sitting perfectly still, demanding that no one touch me, and informing my companions what morons they were (in Christian love) – I came to view that advice as dumb.

We learn the easy way or the hard way. My Inner Mess latches on to the hard way every time.

When my wife and I were rearing our first baby, a friend counseled, 'A full tummy is a happy tummy.' That turned out to be smart advice.

Full, good. Overstuffed, bad.

The drive to satisfy your appetites is a second basic need.

But what if your life story is punctuated by experiences of abject *scarcity*? What happens if you've never felt adequately fed, clothed, sheltered and cuddled?

What happens is that your Inner Brat takes your 'satisfy me' drive into receivership. That's when you give birth to appetites *without an off-switch*.

You don't eat until you're full; you eat until you're stuffed. Or you diet until you're stick thin.

This goes for sexual appetites, too. Instead of an integral part of a mature, marital relationship, your Inner Brat turns sex into an emotional playground from hell. One-night stands. Affairs. Pornography. Sex addiction. Voyeurism. Sexual exploitation. Serial monogamy. Inner Mess sex is *depersonalized* sex. It only bonds you to a stranger, an image, a fantasy. It hurts, but you can't find the off-switch.

Your Inner Brat gets hold of your spiritual appetites too. According to God's design, your spirit grows satisfied, in Christ, *over time*. But time is one commodity a brat can't stomach. Your Inner Brat demands *instant* spiritual gratification. You become addicted to spiritual experiences and religious carnival shows.

It could be Christianized experiences, such as extremist faith healers or health-and-wealth preachers. Or it could be pagan experiences, such as horoscopes and Wicca conventions. It makes no difference. You want satisfaction and you want it now.

Too bad God doesn't work that way. He's really old and he never hurries.

What happens when the mother of all scarcities – money – suckles your Inner Brat? A brat, by definition, can't be satisfied. Neither can your Inner Brat. So either you'll have piles of money and still feel poor, or your Inner Mess will make sure that you never have piles of money to begin with. Either way, you still feel broke.

Paul warned against becoming the kind of people 'whose god is their belly' (Philippians 3:19). Your Inner Brat deifies your 'satisfy me' need.

There's a better way to be satisfied.

God promises that 'he satisfies the longing soul' (Psalm 107:9). You just have to learn how to *ask* both God and the people he has placed around you.

Accept Me!

A guy named Phil started hanging around me. I met him at my church. Suddenly he thought he was my best friend. Phil was a nice guy. Short. Round. Outgoing. But we had different interests and styles. I did my best to welcome Phil into my life, but he didn't help matters.

Phil tried too hard to be accepted. He laughed too loud. Spoke too much. Dominated conversations, and made himself the center of attention. He just showed up wherever I went. He climbed into cars with me without asking. Phil latched onto me.

I started avoiding him. Phil had huge 'accept me' needs.

Yes, I follow Jesus. And, yes, we are called to love others, especially people who make it hard. But Hollywood has made a fortune making disturbing movies about people seeking acceptance, who try to hide it. As a Christian and a pastor, I loved Phil; I wanted the best for him. I knew he desperately wanted to fit in somewhere.

I just had to help him find the right 'somewhere'.

Here's how your Inner Brat might ask to be accepted:

- Being pathetic or overly needy
- Being judgmental
- Using guilt and shame
- Manipulation
- Latching on
- Redefining yourself: wearing masks to please others
- Being phony, obsequious or too eager to please
- Demanding time and attention
- Trying too hard to fit in
- Taking revenge on those who don't accept you.

You may already wonder how I'm going to fit 'you have not because you ask not' into our need for acceptance. It seems so utterly pathetic to go around asking, 'Will you accept me?' There's no way that I want to be on either end of that question.

But wasn't that, in reality, Phil's problem? Wasn't his whole life a pathetic plea for acceptance?

Actually, the 'you have not because you ask not' wisdom of James does apply here, but it's just not as blunt.

The way to ask honestly and cleanly for acceptance is pretty simple. *Get involved in activities that you truly enjoy.* Clubs, sports, classes, museums, church. Create a life for yourself. Don't target a person or even a group of people. Target your heart's desires. Target your interests. Target your God-given calling.

In the process of seeking what you love and enjoy – in the process of accepting yourself – you discover friends. Our men's group started coaching Phil in this direction. He took it to heart. He joined a group that played volleyball and started making friends.

The last time I saw Phil he was happily married, a father, and contentedly connected with his inner life and his outer world.

Help me!

Bad friends. Bad Christians. After all I've done for them! As moving day approached, I had not asked, so I did not have. I was moving an apartment full of belongings and furniture to my new home, and I had not lined up even one friend to help. I assumed they knew I was moving, and if they were real friends, they would have volunteered.

Afterwards, I discovered that my friends assumed I had all the help I needed because I wasn't asking.

My Inner Brat asked for me. Not with a noble, straightforward request, but with a few well-timed whimpers mingled with self-pity and feigned confusion. It worked. Peter rescued me by enlisting a bunch of friends to move me.

That was a masterful stroke of genius by my Inner Mess and it was not pleasing to God.

To say 'help me' is to admit that you're a frail, flailing human. Welcome aboard. If you're too proud to ask for help once in a while, you're too proud. Plus you're too good for God and you're disqualified for grace; flawed humans only need apply.

Unless you'd rather have your Inner Brat do your asking through:

- Manipulation
- Whining
- Demanding
- Dominating
- Clinging
- Acting desperate
- Stealing
- Threatening
- Becoming a loner
- Feeling sorry for yourself
- Blaming
- Being pushy.

I've tried them all and they all work. Somehow, though, when the job is done, I didn't feel that I'd been truly *helped*. I felt that I'd been coddled and humored and tolerated.

Taking No for an Answer

The beginning of entitlement is the end of grace.

I've officiated at enough weddings to see the Inner Brat unleashed in moments of high stress. I even had to enter a woman's rest room and coax a bride out of a locked stall. She had locked her sobbing self inside, five minutes before the wedding, because she discovered six horrifying spots on her gown. Her whole wedding was *ruined*.

Actually, the spots were on the fluffy, bloomer-like undergarments – I am unapologetically too proud to ask for help on the right word here – each one smaller than this letter 'e', light grey in color, and utterly invisible to everybody except an adventurer exploring the inner recesses of her bloomers.

She was normally a very easy-going, fun person. But her brat picked her wedding day – not an uncommon thing – to indulge a queenly hissy fit.

She had dreamed of a perfect wedding day.

Six virtually invisible spots told her *No*.

One of the greatest steps forward you will ever take is when you learn to take No for an answer, and to do so with confidence in yourself and God. You don't need to fall apart. That's because, in his grace, God guarantees to supply your real needs, just in time, through someone else if he chooses or through manna from heaven if he must. Even on your wedding day.

Maybe your friends or family tell you *No* because you're not ready. Maybe they say *No* because they don't trust you, or like you, or want to help you. Maybe you're just not his type or her type. Maybe they're too overwhelmed with their own troubles to pitch in. Their *No* doesn't mean you have to sever the relationship, pout, or get bratty.

If you can't take *No* for an answer, you're not asking, you're demanding, and James says, 'You ask and do not receive because you ask amiss.'

The world has enough brats. Don't you be one too. Don't be crooked. Be straight about your basic needs. Don't force the people around you to guess your wants and needs. Tell them.

At the same time, recognize that they don't owe you.

Even more importantly, recognize that you owe them: 'Owe no one anything except to love one another' (Romans 13:8).

Why is this so important?

Because it's part of gracing your inner mess. Bring your needs into relationship without shame or apology.

That'll keep the trash inside from piling up and spoiling the good times outside.

Taking Out the Trash
....

Have you spotted any brats in your life lately?

During your formative years, which of the four basic needs were your parents or guardians *best* at meeting? *Worst* at meeting (notice me, satisfy me, accept me, help me)? How do your early unmet needs affect your life today?

What do you think Bill means by saying, 'The beginning of entitlement is the end of grace'?

Describe some encounters in which a friend or family member wouldn't take *No* for an answer. How did that encounter affect your relationship?

Is it wrong or unhealthy to have needs? Is it wrong or unhealthy to express them? Why or why not?

In your opinion, when does a person cross the line between a healthy expression of needs and a bratty one?

What does Philippians 4:19 teach about your needs? 'And my God shall supply all your need according to His riches in glory by Christ Jesus.' What *instruments* might God use to do this?

Prayer: For God to fill the gaps left by your earthly father and mother.

Chapter 7
Your Inner Thug

'First we practice sin, then defend it, then boast of it.'
Thomas Manton, 1620–77

Scott almost forgot about driving as he watched Jason's soap opera unfold. The woman had obviously chased down the bus. Scott had some theories about the tube of lipstick she'd held up. It was all coming together now. The stressed-out look on Jason's face. The pony-tailed woman waving Jason back down. Her troubled glance at the hooker and her quizzical look at Jason.

Scott inched forward as it dawned on him that one of his passengers was about to face the fury of a woman scorned.

He had no clue that an even greater fury was about to be unleashed.

The woman walked toward Jason without taking her eyes off him. Jason's head hung down. His hands covered his face.

The woman never saw it coming. As she passed the tract lady, the tattooed felon opposite her shot out his arm. He laughed – more of a snarl really – as he wrapped his arm around the woman's waist and jerked her off her feet and across his lap. The woman screamed and fell toward the window. Her shoulder hit the window. She kicked her legs in a futile attempt to break free.

'Come on, babe. Have some fun with a real man.' The felon forced his face against hers, trying to kiss her mouth.

The bag lady wailed something incomprehensible. She shut her eyes and kept her lips moving though no sound came out. The old man covered his face and huddled against his window.

Scott locked the brakes, tripped his emergency call switch, and jumped out of his seat. At the same instant, Jason yelled, 'Katie!' He lunged across the aisle toward the felon. He fell, grabbing the felon's right arm on his way down. The felon shook him off easily. He kicked Jason in the ribs.

Katie twisted free, landing on her hands and knees. The tract lady stepped over her to beat the felon's head with her handbag. He sent her flying with an elbow to the rib cage; she cried out and fell backward into her seat. He laughed.

Jason scrambled to his feet and lurched on top of him. With both hands he pulled the felon's head downward and began striking his face with his right knee. He connected hard on his second try and blood spattered his coat and the felon's face. The felon cursed and landed a blow in Jason's gut. Jason gasped. He doubled over and fought to breathe. He staggered back into the aisle and into Scott.

The felon took his opportunity to stand. He growled as his off-balance kick glanced off of Katie's shoulder. She scrambled on hands and knees toward the back of the bus and clambered to her feet.

Blood poured from the felon's nose. He took three steps toward the rear exit and pulled the red emergency-exit knob. The doors swung open.

Not fast enough.

As Scott reached the chaos, his martial-arts instincts kicked in. He grabbed the felon by his jacket and pulled him backwards. The felon tumbled into Scott's arms. In a flash, Scott stretched his right arm over the felon's shoulder and around his throat. He placed his hand on his own left bicep, and bent his left arm upward to grab the felon's head from the rear and push it forward.

A chokehold Scott had practiced many times and hoped he'd never have to use.

The felon kicked and tried to turn around, but his head was immobilized. He tried to nail Scott with his elbows, but Scott held him too close. He couldn't break free. He couldn't breathe, either. Pressure from Scott's v-shaped right arm restricted blood flow to the felon's brain. Moments later his eyelids fluttered and he passed out.

Scott let him drop to the floor.

The bus looked like a battlefield. Jason moved toward his sobbing wife. The bag lady's lips moved in ongoing dialogue with her inner demons. The tract lady brushed off her skirt and blazer. She gathered the scattered contents of her purse and glared with satisfaction at the felon's crumpled frame.

Scott heard a distant siren. With this traffic they'll take forever to get here.

A sudden commotion made Scott realize he didn't have forever. The hooker had jumped out of her seat with a muffled scream. Scott followed her eyes to what every inner-city bus driver dreaded – what every bus driver's spouse prayed against.

The young punk who'd been sleeping next to the hooker had pulled out a gun. His shaking hand pointed it in the general direction of Scott's head.

* * *

A Horrible Day at the Office

Him (shouting): 'Don't you ever do that to me again! If I tell you to come here, you do it now. I mean right away. Don't you ever make me wait for you again, or you've had it. Do you understand me? I said, DO YOU UNDERSTAND ME? Now get over here right now, shut up and listen!'

Me: a scrawny seventeen-year-old clerk in a busy photo-finishing store.

Him: my hefty boss, Don, chewing me out at the top of his lungs.

The Setting: Almost a hundred impatient customers – most of them professional photographers – waiting for their number to be called in a cramped store on a wet, snowy Chicago evening. Eight or nine clerks like me worked behind a long glass counter, handing finished enlargements to customers and collecting their money. I had two customers on the phone and one in the store. Don summoned me. I told him to wait a minute.

That was a big mistake.

Every head in the store turned to watch Don chew me out till his middle-aged, blotchy face glowed red and my teenage eyes fought back tears.

He was the worst person I'd ever met. He was always mean. Don generated his own climate: a cloud of unhappiness went before him and dreariness followed after him. We stayed out of his way as much as we could. No one wanted to be on the receiving end of anything he had to say.

Some people have the gift of inflicting pain. They criticize. Complain. Find fault. Spread rumors. Question motives. Create strife. They have a very active Inner Thug.

They populate some churches I know.

And depopulate them too.

The saddest part is they never see their own meanness. To them, it's righteousness. To their neighbors, it's nastiness.

Paul warned, 'But if you bite and devour one another, beware lest you be consumed by one another!' (Galatians 5:15). Solomon counseled, 'A perverse man sows strife, and a whisperer separates the best of friends' (Proverbs 16:28).

Your Inner Thug sows strife. Sometimes it's surreal: you watch your thug push away your spouse or kids, and regret it even as you do it.

The Bible lays out a nice, three-step descent into relational carnage.

Three Steps Down

*Let us not become conceited, provoking one another,
envying one another.*

(Galatians 5:26)

Conceited

Step one. *Conceited.* The original Greek word means 'full of
empty glory.' It indicates boasting about stuff that just doesn't
matter. This is the kind of conceit that makes you feel better
than others. Your Inner Thug says, 'I'm better than you.'

A healthy person would reply, 'Maybe you are. But does
it matter?'

It matters to your Inner Mess.

Answer this question: *In what ways are you better than your
spouse and your closest friends?* Authentically better. Are you
smarter? Stronger? Better-looking? Kinder? More generous?
More disciplined? Wealthier? Cleaner? Tougher? Better
dressed? Less complicated? Name the top two or three ways.
Don't be proud and don't be humble; just be true.

If you can't answer, it's safe to assume you have channeled
your 'better than you' drive into Inner Mess territory. So,
consider instead how you are *worse* than your spouse or
friends. This is your flesh's twisted way of making you better
than others. So, what is it? I'm better than you at failing? At
being useless? At being too fat? Stupid? Hating myself? I've
suffered more than you? I've achieved less than anybody else
in the family?

In a creepy twist, your Inner Mess revels in your being
better at being worse. Your Inner Mess relishes its role as
martyr.

So ask yourself how you are better (or worse) than your
spouse and best friends.

Then ask this follow-up question: *When my Inner Mess is
active, how do I prove that I'm better than others?* This drive to be

better is a cousin to your need to be noticed. We never lose the childhood dream of being somebody's hero. God created us in his image; we're made to reflect his glory. That happens when we let our strengths and gifts shine through.

It is not conceited to embrace your gifts. It is not conceited to enjoy them and use them to better your life, your family, your church, and your world. It is not conceited to identify what makes you special and to take satisfaction in it.

It is conceited when you routinely make yourself the central topic of conversation. One pastor I know can't stop talking about himself. He loads conversations with stories about his childhood and his ministry in the past. He works himself into every success story in his church. His boasting comes out of a need to be noticed. Even his self-deprecating stories make him sound better at being self-deprecating. Conceit.

It is also conceited when you use your strengths to minimize the strengths of others. Or when you use your suffering to invalidate the suffering of others.

A woman in my church who had been deeply wounded told me, 'You don't know what I'm feeling. You haven't gone through what I've been through.' I responded that she didn't need to invalidate my experiences in order to validate her own. Moreover, she didn't know my life. She didn't know what I'd been through. Actually, I *did* know what she was feeling – our lives had more parallels than she realized. And even though I hadn't gone through her exact experience, I'd gone through an analogous experience and knew what that pain felt like.

Conceit is the empty boasting of your Inner Thug. It is the part of you that responds to stress by pounding down the people around you. It is the first step downward to relational carnage.

Provoking one another

The 1967 heavyweight boxing title match pitted champion Muhammad Ali against challenger Ernie Terrell.1 Ali had changed his name from Cassius Clay: 'Cassius Clay is a slave name,' he once said. 'I didn't choose it, and I didn't want it. I am Muhammad Ali, a free name – it means beloved of God – and I insist people use it when speaking to me and of me.'[2]

Throughout the pre-match hype, Ernie Terrell kept calling him Cassius Clay. When they finally stepped into the ring, Terrell still taunted him, calling him Cassius Clay.

When Muhammad Ali knocked Ernie Terrell to the mat, he stood over him taunting, 'What's my name, fool? What's my name?'

Provoking one another. It makes sense in a boxing ring. It doesn't make sense in daily life.

Guys call this a 'pissing contest', Women call it 'being catty', You needlessly sow strife. *Conceit* says, 'I'm better than you.' *Provoking one another* means, 'Now let me prove it.' So you pound others down – but not blatantly. Instead, you might compare salaries, batting averages, bicep size, gun size, jewelry collections, cooking abilities or children's SATs. You drive the flashiest cars, wear the gaudiest diamonds and live in the biggest house. You validate yourself through sexual conquests and actually keep count. I had a friend who had reached 365 sex partners, the number of days in the year.

You're also in the deepest debt, but that's for chapter fourteen.

You compare yourself with friends, not to celebrate their achievement but to claim the 'better than' trophy as your own. Your Inner Thug can't stop talking trash.

Ali won by a decision.

But what happens when you lose? What happens when you can't prove that you're better than the next guy? What then? That's when your Inner Thug shifts strategies.

Envying one another

Envy is the disgruntled feeling you get when you realize you're not better than others, and it ticks you off. Your conceit has been tested and wounded. Now you feel pain toward yourself and malignancy toward your friends for their success or happiness.

Maybe Scottie Pippen envied the recently commissioned seventeen-foot-tall bronze sculpture of the retired Michael Jordan, soon to stand as a tribute in front of Chicago's United Center.

Maybe Ernie Terrell envied Muhammad Ali's title and championship belt.

Maybe Don, my boss, envied the fact that I was young and starting out in life and he was middle-aged, overweight and about to pop a vein.

Maybe I envied a local mega-church pastor and his explosive church growth and international adulation. To my spirit – my Noble Self – it was all for the kingdom of God. But to my Inner Mess, that nearby pastor was trespassing on my kingdom.

Maybe you envy your sister who got her third promotion while you're still changing diapers, or your neighbor for buying a new car every year while you nurse yours along with over 150,000 miles. Or you envy your child-free neighbor because your kids keep you too tired to exercise, and now your husband is surrounded by shapely assistants while you morph into the frump you always mocked.

How different are we from the bad guys in this verse? 'For he [Pontius Pilate] knew that the chief priests had handed Him [Jesus] over because of envy' (Mark 15:10).

No wonder the Bible teaches that relationship breakdown – led by envy – is a sure sign of a flesh-dominated life (1 Corinthians 3:3). That's what happens when your Inner Mess hijacks your life.

A popular children's game has kids pounding little mole heads as soon as they pop out of a hole. Your Inner Thug does the same thing; it pounds down other people to make you feel better about yourself.

It's especially fun when you play as a team. A young pastor told me about a two-hour board meeting that was nothing but 'character assassination'. The board members – most of them older than their 29-year-old pastor – ganged up on him. My hunch is that they envied their new pastor's popularity and feared he would take their fiefdom from them. So they teamed up for a good pounding.

A secret society operating in India from the thirteenth to the nineteenth century gives us the word *thug*. The Thugee cult worshiped Kali, the goddess of death and destruction. They practiced ritual assassination, usually by strangling their victim with a yellow scarf in honor of Kali. Thugees killed without remorse; assassination was a holy act. So was confiscating the wealth of their victims. The British government stamped them out in the nineteenth century.

They missed a few church board members.

They missed the thug ensconced in the back of my bus, too.

An Identity Crisis

Conceit, provoking one another, envy. The three-step descent to relational hell. All three steps have one quality in common: *they mutate relationships into a competitive sport.*

Why?

Because your Inner Mess bases your self-worth on being better than others. You have to compete and win to feel good about yourself.

Why?

Because you are sleepwalking through an identity crisis. If you do not feel secure in your real identity, your Inner Mess will create a new one for you – always at the expense of others. Your Inner Thug claws its way to the top. You may win the gold medal, but you'll leave broken hearts in your wake.

And you might not even realize it.

Christians believe that our identity – apart from Christ – suffers a serious malfunction. Ever since Adam and Eve's moral indiscretion, the flesh rules the roost. Of all the parts of your soul, it is the chief. The Bible calls this 'being in the flesh'. For example:

- 'So then, those who are in the flesh cannot please God' (Romans 8:8).
- 'For when we were in the flesh, the sinful passions which were aroused by the law were at work in our members to bear fruit to death' (Romans 7:5).

Your Inner Mess pulled a palace coup, and now occupies the throne. You don't just *have* an Inner Mess, you *are* one. Your core identity is a distorted version of God's original design.

Your flesh knocked you to the mat and stood over your soul demanding, 'What's my name, fool? What's my name?' It pulled an identity switch. Instead of a holy child of God, created in his image, the flesh tagged you as a gang-banger tags the liquor store: it tagged you a child of the flesh (Romans 9:8), a child of a slave (Galatians 4:30), a child of disobedience (Ephesians 5:6) and a child of the devil (1 John 3:10). Somewhere in the mêlée you got a new last name, a royally messed-up new identity.

That new identity represents a corruption of your God-given identity. It is a web of interlocking lies and unrealities spun into your core consciousness.

Your Inner Mess defines you with a host of warped 'I am' statements: I am no good. I am a wretch. I am meant to be used and tossed aside. I am worthless. I am bad. I am not worth loving. I am never going to amount to anything.

On the flipside, when your Inner Mess self-identifies as a minor deity, your 'I am' statements sound like this: I am entitled – the world owes me. I am accountable to no one. I am a free moral agent. I am on my own. I am a self-made person. I am my own boss. I am good enough for God.

Before your Inner Thug ever does a number on anybody else, it does a number on you. While you were sleeping, your Inner Thug switched your I.D. tags. That is the root of humanity's identity crisis. Your fallen nature defines you. It paints its own macabre self-portrait on the corridors of your mind.

And that is why we bite and devour one another. Your Inner Mess trashes your outer world at will, because it's been trashing your inner world all your life. It's king or queen of the world.

And that is why it is so hard to change. As long as your Inner Mess sits on the throne of your life, it won't let you flip an 'off switch' on bad habits, addictions and hang-ups. You are 'in the flesh'.

And that is why we need a new identity and a new nature, which God so mercifully provides to all who believe and ask.

And that is why we have to hurry to the part of this book that talks about redemption. But we still have one more chapter before we turn that corner. Hang in with me.

Taking Out the Trash

··

When have you been on the receiving end of another person's Inner Thug? How did it affect you? How long did the effects remain?

Have you caught yourself unleashing your Inner Thug against anyone lately? What happened? What was God's opinion of the episode?

Think of someone in your life who is conceited. What, in your opinion, motivates that conceit? How does that conceit provoke conflict? Envy?

How much do you agree or disagree with the idea that the Inner Mess constitutes the core identity of people in their natural state? What do Ephesians 2:1–3 and Titus 3:3, 4 say about this?

Prayer: For the honesty to admit and the grace to transform in your Inner Thug.

Chapter 8
Your C.I.A. Agent

'The hypocrite doth veil and smother his sin.'
Thomas Watson (1620–86)

'Everybody shut up! You, sit down. Sit down!'

Scott held up his hands and backed into a seat. *God, help us. Take care of my kids. Take care of my wife.*

'You,' he said, looking at the drunken couple, 'shut up. Sit down. Everybody!' The punk waved his still-shaking gun at the passengers. The felon groaned as he regained consciousness. He shook his groggy head and fought to focus his eyes. The first thing he saw clearly was the gun. His eyes got narrow. He clambered back into his seat, holding his nose. It was smashed and swollen. Blood ran over his lips and dripped off his chin. He cursed and shook his head.

The punk was so stoned that anything could happen. Scott hoped that everybody would just give him what he wanted and get him off the bus – no heroics.

Katie and Jason found seats and leaned against each other. Jason's left eye started to swell. He still wasn't breathing right. Katie sat expressionless and gray.

The punk threw the trembling hooker his baseball cap. 'Everybody – money in the hat. Now!'

The hooker started collecting money. Some of the passengers hesitated. 'All of it!' The tract lady scowled as she nursed her bruised ribs and poured the contents of her change purse into the cap. The felon dropped in a crumpled wad of bills. The old man next to him huddled into his corner and quaked; the hooker passed him by.

She worked her way toward the front. The hat got full fast.

'Bring me the hat! Bring me the hat! *Now*!'

A middle-aged man caught Scott's eye. He sat in the back row, two seats from the gunman. The man opened his jacket enough to reveal a badge. The city had begun an undercover ride-along program. Not even the drivers knew when a cop was on board. Scott's heart skipped a beat as the cop's hand slid inside his jacket. The cop tilted his head at the punk and sneered.

No! Don't be a hero! Scott clenched his jaw and gave a slight shake of his head. The cop nodded his head *yes* and began withdrawing his hand. Scott's heart pounded. His chest tightened with dread. *Idiot!*

The hooker returned with the hat full of money. The punk grabbed it and tore toward the open back door. The sirens were closer now.

He reached the top step, next to Scott, as the undercover cop stood and pointed a gun at his back.

'Drop your weapon!'

The punk whirled and lifted his gun. As if in slow motion, Scott saw the tattooed felon hurl his body against the punk. He listened in horror as a shot rang out.

Then a second shot.

Blood sprayed the windows as two human forms crumpled to the floor.

* * *

Don't Ask, Don't Tell

The server at a local coffee shop called out, 'Pastor Bill, I have your low-carb blended mocha, triple-shot decaf ready.' I cringed. Not at the shame of ordering a drink that was both low-carb and decaf. But at the server blowing my cover.

She leaked my secret identity as a pastor to the whole coffee shop. What's the matter with her? Doesn't she know that loose lips sink ships? Being a pastor embarrasses me.

Maybe it's because I know that I'm not worthy of the title. Maybe it's because people immediately raise their defenses when they find out what I do. Maybe it's because many people think pastors are nerdy, though I know that the opposite is true. Most of the pastors I've met have been dedicated, genuine, highly trained leaders. I believe that pastors are God's gift to the world. I value the office of a pastor. Just don't 'out' me as one of them.

That's my secret to reveal in my own time. And don't go shaking your judgmental head at me unless you have no high-cringe-factor secrets of your own.

Furtively darting from seat to seat, a clandestine operative at the back of your bus has sworn an oath to keep your secrets or die trying. He is your Inner C.I.A. Agent. After Adam and Eve ate the forbidden fruit, they covered themselves with fig leaves and they hid. Humankind has been covering up and hiding ever since.

When God asked Adam why he was hiding, Adam said, 'I heard Your voice in the garden, and I was afraid because I was naked; and I hid myself' (Genesis 3:10). Huh? He'd been naked all his life. What was different now?

He had never before been naked *and* ashamed. This shame drove him into hiding. It also sparked a comedy of blame-shifting.

Adam blamed God. Then he blamed Eve. Then Eve blamed the serpent. The serpent had nobody. No matter what other survival tactic your Inner Mess may employ, its primary *modus operandi* is to toss your partner overboard if that's what it takes to survive.

The fall – the theological name for sin's entrance into the world of humanity – trashed Adam's relationship with Eve, Eve's relationship with Adam, and God's relationship with them both. It shattered the linkages that held them together; it shattered their internal linkages to their own identities. It called down the very results that God had promised: death and decay. It gave birth to that innate and universal twist called the Adamic nature, which we know as the flesh or the Inner Mess. The flesh then gathered all the fragments of guilt, shame, evil, pride, rebellion and sin lurking in the human heart and locked them in a vault hoping they would just go away. They didn't.

And they won't. No matter how much you hide. No matter how hard you try to keep them secret. Your C.I.A. Agent can never defy the fundamental laws of relational survival.

Laws of Relational Survival

> *Therefore a man shall leave his father and mother and be joined to his wife, and they shall become one flesh. And they were both naked, the man and his wife, and were not ashamed.*
>
> (Genesis 2:24, 25)

The Law of Differentiation

If you were a fan of the 1990s sitcom *Seinfeld*, you might laugh at George Costanza, but deep inside, isn't there a part of you that relates? In one episode, George idolizes a new friend, nicknamed Cool Tony. George suggests that he and Cool Tony go bowling. Tony suggests rock-climbing instead, and turns around his baseball cap. George offers to make sandwiches for the trip and turns around his cap, too. Later, Jerry teases George about having a man-crush on Tony. George replies that Tony was the first cool guy he'd ever been friends with in his whole life.

Pathetic? George latched onto Cool Tony as Phil latched onto me. Like I've latched onto others in my life. My hunch is that you have, too. We have all broken the Law of Differentiation.

110

Genesis introduces the Law of Differentiation with the phrase 'and they were both naked.' The Hebrew word translated 'both' is the normal word for the number two. Moses literally wrote, 'And they were, the *two* of them, naked.' This is important because the next verse says they became *one* flesh.

The Law of Differentiation teaches that, no matter how tight a relationship may be, you never become the other person, and you never lose yourself in the other person.

When Margi and I lit our unity candle at our wedding, we left both side candles burning. It was our way of symbolizing that, while we were creating a union, we were still distinct individuals. Don't take this as a criticism of the world's side-candle-blowers. It was just our little way of honoring one another's identity.

Okay, okay. Maybe it is a criticism: I am way, way better than you.

Your Inner Mess is always on the prowl for a decent identity. *Who am I? Which version of me will people like?* Since your fallen identity is so embarrassing to your Inner Mess, it creates new identities. Not through forging linkages to Christ, but through oozing into enmeshed relationships – codependent, manipulative, smothering, controlling, care-taking, clinging relationships.

If you just feel like a great big Nobody unless you're latching on to a great big Somebody, you have a problem with the Law of Differentiation. And anybody with even half a life will run the other way when they see you coming.

Adam and Eve were two. Healthy relationships keep it that way.

The Law of Transparency
Moses also tells us that Adam and Eve were naked. 'Naked' comes into English from the old English verb *to nake*. 'To nake' meant to strip. You could nake the bark from a tree or the paint from a table. Naked (one syllable) means stripped.

Exposed. Uncovered.

That's how Adam and Eve were in the Garden of Eden. No clothes, no problem. In the very next line, Moses talks about shame, a function of the inner life, so Moses intends his readers to go a little deeper than physical nakedness. Adam and Eve were not only naked physically, they were naked emotionally too. This is the Law of Transparency.

Under this law, for intimate relationships to work, you have to strip yourself of pretense and masks in the presence of another. You have to expose yourself fully to another. This sets off deafening alarms at the back of your bus.

When I was growing up, my relatives taught me, 'Never air your dirty laundry.' The Inner Mess shouts *Amen!* It shudders at the thought that you might reveal some of your inner garbage dump to outsiders. It enlists an army of allies to keep your dirty little secrets.

Overseeing the secrecy operations, your C.I.A. Agent has conned you into thinking that your flaws and wounds make you unlovable. That stuff is CLASSIFIED. The underlying problem is the fear of rejection.

That is a valid fear.

Old-fashioned diners often offered a 'blue-plate special'. You could select from two or three dinners at a discount price, with one condition. No substitutions. If you order the roast beef, you get mashed potatoes and peas. Even if you don't like peas. You can't ask for corn instead. No substitutions.

In the universe of love and intimacy, everybody's a blue-plate special. We all have peas or Brussels sprouts or wilted spinach on our plates. *Something* stinks out the joint. If you are going to love me, you have to love me broccoli and all, or else I won't feel authentically loved. And unless I show you my whole plate, I'll always have a nagging suspicion that, when my blood sausages leak out, you'll run away screaming as if you're being chased by a tax auditor.

Your Inner Mess throws a napkin over your wilted spinach and hopes the diner won't notice.

Under the Law of Transparency, you offer yourself to your friend, partner, spouse and lover as a blemished, flawed, broken-in-places, authentic, human package deal. Either someone gets the whole plate or they get none of it.

No hiding stuff.

Let me quickly say that I'm not telling you to blab your secrets to everybody you meet. That kind of attention-seeking is equally from the flesh. I'm suggesting that you cultivate a handful of close friendships so you can put your worst crud on the table and know that you are still loved.

The Law of Shame

My pastor preached to our Sunday-morning crowd in his sepulchral voice: 'Most of your friends and family are going to spend eternity in hell.' He paused. 'And most of you don't give a damn!'

Then he paused again to let us shift uncomfortably in our already uncomfortable seats. He continued in artificial tones:

'And most of you are more disturbed that I, your pastor, just said "damn" than that your friends are going to hell.'

We all looked at our toes with faces full of appropriate shame.

He looked satisfied.

No wonder people increasingly dislike the church but love Jesus. Sometimes the church gives off the vibe of a gigantic, wagging, foam finger of shame.

I'm sorry.

Moses tells us that Adam and Eve 'were not ashamed'. Let's make sure we have our terms straight, because guilt and shame are not the same.

Guilt. Guilt is the feeling you get when you've done something wrong or hurtful. Picture an ultra-sensitive Mother Superior on your bus, filling simmering pots of guilt, and ladling out big bowls whenever the need arises. Call this character Conscience. Be thankful you have one. If you don't have a conscience, seek professional help. Be even more thankful your neighbor has one. Be most thankful your spouse has one. Your conscience comes pre-wired with an innate sense of God's laws (Romans 2:15).

Even so, it's not an infallible guide. As I mentioned, my conscience ladled out heavy doses of guilt when I first saw *Star Wars*, just for sitting in a movie theater. Today I consider that false guilt. My conscience needed a biblical makeover. Every conscience does.

The conscience is especially tuned to *relationships*. That's a good thing. The guilt you feel when you damage a relationship motivates two non-optional pursuits. One is the pursuit of justice – somebody has to balance the scales. The second is the pursuit of reconciliation.

The pursuit of justice. For a Christian who's firing on all cylinders, the pursuit of justice drives you back to Ground Zero with Jesus; back to that amazing day when it first hit you that his death balanced God's scales of justice on your behalf. Guilt guides you back to the cross, mentally speaking, so you can remember that whatever punishment you deserved was already endured by Christ. It motivates you to use God's gracious resources to renew your fellowship with him. We'll discuss this more in chapters ten and fourteen.

Because of the cross, you walk away clean with God. The pressure's off as far as you and God are concerned.

The pursuit of reconciliation. This makes the second pursuit – reconciliation – immeasurably easier. You can reconcile your fractured friendship without denying, explaining, blaming, excusing, rationalizing or being defensive, because your conscience is no longer nagging you about *divine* retribution. Rightly used, guilt keeps your Inner Mess in check. But what if guilt isn't rightly used? What if guilt creates more alienation in your life than reconciliation? That's when your soul mutates from guilt into shame.

Shame. Jesus' death means that you can make peace with people you've hurt *without punishing yourself*. Healthy reconciliation does not involve punishment. It does not include putting yourself down, loathing yourself, groveling, paying a price, or any other self-punishment technique. It does, however, include restitution. But no amount of restitution can ever undo your harmful act. That's why reconciliation, properly pursued, never includes self-denigration; that would just be your Inner Saint run amok.

Your Inner Mess weeps tears of joy whenever it hears you speak forth your self-abhorrent putdowns: 'I'm such a jerk. I hate myself. I'm no good. I'm not worthy of you. I don't know why you stay with a loser like me.' Picture your Inner Mess applauding every syllable. Why do we do this?

Because our flesh maintains a cynical skepticism about the efficacy of Christ's death; if he didn't balance the scales of justice, we'll just have to balance them ourselves.

No relationship can be strong if either partner indulges in self-loathing.

The great divide between guilt and shame is whether or not you torment yourself for your failures. Adam and Eve were naked – as they had been all their lives – but now, for the first time ever, they were also ashamed. They judged themselves unworthy of being in community with God. So far, so good: they were indeed guilty and unworthy of God.

But then they covered themselves and hid: that's when shame took over. Their attempt at self-punishment didn't accomplish anything except to delay their reconciliation with God.

Shame plays the same game today. Under the Law of Shame, you judge yourself to be unworthy of relationship, intimacy and love. You therefore sentence yourself – or parts of yourself – to solitary confinement. You might not even be aware of it. Your flesh sabotages your marriage, your dating life, and your friendships. It spoils your friendship with God. It makes you crazy.

Shame is like rocket fuel for your Inner Mess. If you have a track record of relationship malfunctions, could it be that you violate the law of shame?

Who's to blame for that?

Nobody Can Shame You But You

What a stellar moment it was one chilly evening when I refused to let a church lady dump her load of shame on me. She accosted me because I was a pastor and I hadn't visited a distant relative of hers in the hospital. This modern-day Pharisee – with her bun wound so tightly that it made her nose fat – had worked herself up into a self-righteous huff. Neither the hospitalized man nor the bun-headed church lady was part of my church. Moreover, our church's philosophy called for everyday Christians to make those hospital calls, not pastors.

Even so, this stern woman picked the occasion of somebody else's funeral service to scold me over how appalled she was that I, a pastor, hadn't visited the hospital. She got to me right as I entered the chapel. I thought she was just saying hello. It took some moments before my mind registered that the look on her face was not a cordial smile but a frosty grimace.

When it sank in, my eyes grew wide and I couldn't believe she was accosting me at a funeral.

Normally, I would have crumbled. Normally, I would have apologized for my non-offense and flogged myself with delightfully neurotic shame. I would have – as usual – caved in to the relentless pressure of other people's opinions and to my irrational fear of other people's disapproval. But not this time.

This time was different: I was in the process of learning how to stop my Inner Mess from trashing my outer world.

I refused to take in her shame. I shook my head, told the sanctimonious finger-wagger that I hadn't come for this, and walked away. Hah! No floggings today!

What a moment! When the foam finger of shame demanded my attention, I snubbed it. Almost as good as hitting a triple.

Moses said that Adam and Eve were naked but not ashamed. Of 155 occurrences of the word *shame* in the Old Testament, this is the one and only time it appears in the reflexive form. You could translate it this way: *they were naked and they did not shame themselves.* God wove a fundamental law of relational survival into shame's very first biblical appearance: *Shame is something you do to yourself.* Nobody can shame you but you. They can try, but you don't have to take it in.

Secrecy

Shame always pulls you away from intimate relationships. This, you reason, makes it less likely that others will catch a whiff of the Brussels sprouts on your plate. Your shame keeps them at arm's distance. You are safe. But that's not all you are.

You are also alone. This has been the agenda of your C.I.A. Agent all along. It smells the spoiled meat at the back of your bus and pulls a curtain across the aisle. All your life it has toiled to isolate and mask the real you, that it might shield the real you from rejection.

That's too bad, because it has also shielded you against authentic, intimate relationships.

C.S. Lewis wrote the following:

> *There is no safe investment. To love at all is to be vulnerable. Love anything, and your heart will certainly be wrung and possibly be broken. If you want to make sure of keeping it intact, you must give your heart to no one, not even to an animal. Wrap it carefully round with hobbies and little luxuries; avoid all entanglements; lock it up safe in the casket or coffin of your selfishness. But in that casket — safe, dark, motionless, airless — it will change. It will not be broken; it will become unbreakable, impenetrable, irredeemable... The only place outside Heaven where you can be perfectly safe from all the dangers and perturbations of love is Hell. I believe that the most lawless and inordinate loves are less contrary*

to God's will than a self-invited and self-protective lovelessness.[1]

If you appreciate irony, chew on this: the only way your Inner Mess knows how to protect you from the pain of rejection is by rejecting you first.

Just as I rejected my own pastoral identity. It's who I am. When I am dominated by the flesh, I don't even like myself. I shame myself for being a pastor. 'You're only as sick as your secrets,' say the twelve steppers. 'Yes, what joy for those whose record the LORD has cleared of sin, whose lives are lived in complete honesty!' sings the Psalmist (Psalm 32:2, NLT). I want to show you how to send your C.I.A. Agent on an extended vacation to Siberia. You can live in complete honesty – with God, yourself, and at least one other person.

It's time to turn the corner.

Maybe I should start with myself. Go ahead and call me Pastor Bill. Call me Reverend Pastor Bill if you like. Tell the world. It's okay. I still might cringe and worry what others will think. But I refuse to be ashamed of my Inner Pastor.

The other characters will take more doing.

And please don't ask me to say grace at your next dinner party. I may have gone public about being a pastor, but I still like to keep a low profile.

Taking Out the Trash

....

Review the three laws of relational survival: the Law of Differentiation, the Law of Transparency, and the Law of Shame. Which law did your family violate most during your upbringing?

What is your reaction to the idea that reconciliation must not include punishment? Do you think that idea squares with Scripture? Does it square with your Inner Mess?

By now, you might be getting a handle on the many ways in which your flesh has an impact on your life. Identify a few ways in which you've been carnal (flesh-dominated) and not realized it. Please visit our online Inner Mess community at www.innermess.com and share some new discoveries you've made about your own Inner Mess.

How powerful is the force of shame in your life?

How does your Inner Mess react to Ephesians 5:11: 'And have no fellowship with the unfruitful works of darkness, but rather expose them'? How healthy is that response? How does it affect your relationships?

Prayer: That God would bring you to an honest, open life and to a place of freedom from the burden of secret shame.

Part Two

I discovered the steps to handling my Inner Mess out of sequence. It felt like gathering the pieces of a puzzle over many years and never seeing the box top.

Here's the box top.

In Part One we focused on meeting your Inner Mess. My goal was to help you see how your Inner Mess stretches its tentacles into every area of life.

Now that you are thoroughly distressed, we can turn a corner. It's time to get your life back.

In Part Two we'll focus on God's process of ransoming you from a flesh-dominated life. Bible experts call this process *sanctification*. Consider Part Two your enrollment in *Sanctification 101*. In chapters nine to twelve, we'll lay out the puzzle pieces. Then, in chapters thirteen to fifteen, we'll put them all together. It's time to stop your Inner Mess from trashing your outer world.

Chapter 9

Grace

'Grace is more than love; it is love set absolutely free
and made to be a triumphant victor over the righteous
judgment of God against the sinner.'

Lewis Sperry Chafer, 1933

Momentary silence gave way to pandemonium.

Passengers ducked as low as the cramped space allowed.
Some scrambled for the front exit. Another shot stopped them
dead in their tracks.

'Don't move! Nobody move!' screamed the punk. He
shoved the bleeding felon aside and climbed to his feet. He
looked at the fallen cop and swore. 'Oh, man! Nobody was
supposed to get hurt! Why didn't he just listen?'

The hooker felt the cop's neck. 'I think he's alive.
Somebody call for help!' She looked at the punk. 'This guy's
a cop. You shot a cop!'

Scott's mind raced. He wanted nothing more than to get
this punk off the bus. But he didn't want to let a possible cop-
killer escape.

'Where's my money?' The punk scraped together some
bills from the floor and turned toward the rear exit. Scott had
only seconds to react. He made his decision. Somebody else
beat him to it.

As the punk stepped over his body, the felon's bloody
hand shot out and grabbed his ankle. He cursed as he toppled
head over heels. The punk's head hit the edge of the bottom

step with a sickening crack. He lay motionless as the felon pulled himself up.

It's over. Thank God. It's over. Scott reached out to steady the felon.

Without warning, the felon slapped Scott's hand away, stretched down and yanked the gun from the punk's hand. He took steady aim at Katie and staggered toward her.

* * *

> But Jesus looked at them and said, 'With men it is
> impossible, but not with God; for with God all things are
> possible' (Mark 10:27).

A crippled old man moved among listless street people, embracing each one and pleading with them to come with him. Notes of *Amazing Grace* sung by gruff voices filled the crowded chapel. The old man touched each derelict. Drunk. Stoned. Smelling of urine or worse. Infested with lice and fleas. Unshaven. Mentally deranged. He didn't skip anybody. The altar call would not be finished until Harry Saulnier had embraced each man, looked into his eyes and said, 'Friend, God loves you and so do I. You need Jesus. Won't you receive him today? He'll change you. I'll go forward with you. Won't you please receive the Savior?'

The Pacific Garden Mission has kept watch over Chicago's skid row since 1923. One of America's great street missions, the 'Old Lighthouse' has witnessed countless lives unshackled from their Inner Mess. Every night, hundreds of men receive food, shelter, delousing, cleaning, sobering up, education, job training and a message on the love of Christ. I volunteered several times to preach that message. It always scared me.

I was out of my element. I grew up in sheltered, middle-class comfort. I had virtually no experience with drunkenness, drugs, crime and mental illness. I was young – in my mid-twenties – and every time I preached there, I felt like Daniel being thrown to the lions. The ordeal began with prayer. Painful prayer.

As the volunteer speaker for the evening I arrived, as required, an hour early for prayer. I met with a handful of mission workers and the mission's director, Harry Saulnier. Harry had run the mission since 1940. Well into his eighties, he attended most of the services and always joined in the pre-service prayer. I'm all for prayer, but Harry's idea of prayer stretched beyond my endurance.

We prayed in a cramped, chilly backroom. Extra chairs stacked beside extra furniture – it looked like storage room. Concrete floors covered in vinyl tile. Bare light bulbs casting dim shadows. We prayed on our knees. We knelt on those rock-hard floors and cried out to God for the sin-ravaged lives gathering next door. Only minutes into the prayer time, my knees ached. My back ached. I couldn't get comfortable.

Yet kneeling beside me, Harry – an arthritic octogenarian – prayed as if his life depended on it. He was oblivious to the pain, the time, the surroundings. When he wasn't praying, he was cheering on the prayers of others. He volleyed forth a slew of *Amens* and *Hallelujahs*. My body ached to finish, yet Harry kept us praying until we had 'prayed through'.

Later I found out that he had had both knees and hips replaced. He must have prayed too much, I figured.

I felt small.

Today I feel awed and grateful for those meetings in that backroom turned heaven-on-earth.

When Harry felt that we had prayed enough, we began the service. The chapel was always full. The order of service never changed. Singing. Preaching. *Amazing Grace*. Altar call.

And during the altar call, that old man became Jesus. He stepped down from the platform and melded with the people, loving the unlovely. He embraced men who hadn't been touched with kindness as far back as they could remember. Open sores, bad smells, nothing stopped him. Harry embraced street people the way Jesus embraced lepers. Nobody had sunk too low for Harry's love.

Watching Harry sparked a flicker of hope for my Inner Mess. Would Jesus love the derelict parts of my soul the way Harry loved those men?

What Would Jesus Do: Standard Edition

Sanctification is ultimately about our doing what Jesus would do. A sanctified person follows the steps of Jesus. W.W.J.D. (What Would Jesus Do) fervor began in America in 1896 with the classic book *In His Steps*, by Charles M. Sheldon. *In His Steps* has sold over 30 million copies. Sheldon tells the story of how Christians transform their lives and their town when they ask, 'What would Jesus do?' before they make any decisions.

I read *In His Steps* in my early teens, tried to follow its premise, and failed. I thought I was alone. My delusional imagination pictured millions of happy Christians doing what Jesus did, without faltering and without struggling, while I settled for a sub-par spirituality.

I'm not one to quibble with a Christian classic and perennial bestseller. No one can disagree with the book's premise: we who call ourselves Christians should walk in the steps of the Master. You can't read the Bible and argue with that. Plus, Sheldon's book masterfully portrays how our lives and cities would change if we succeeded. But, somehow, I missed exactly how I can succeed at the W.W.J.D. lifestyle, except by willpower alone. Maybe the secret is in the book, but, in my immaturity, I missed it.

For me, the abundant Christian life decomposed into white-knuckled determination and duty. Nothing worked. I couldn't stop my Inner Mess from trashing my outer world. So I did what most frustrated followers of Jesus do.

I resigned.

I resigned myself to a second-rate spirituality and a half-baked holiness. I resigned myself to toughing it out. To sanctification – the kind of holiness that really pleases God – through sheer will power. Suck it up, contain your Inner Mess as much as possible, and fight hard to make myself holy.

A trip to a museum changed all that.

The Rotunda of Witnesses

My skin tingled. I was on the verge of something big. I was standing in the Rotunda of Witnesses and reading a banner. It blazed forth the secret of sanctification and the solution to my Inner Mess. Though it would take some time to sink in, my eyes were opening and I would never look at life with Jesus the same way again.

The Billy Graham Center Museum at Wheaton College offered an escape from the pressures of ministry. I'd go every few months to recharge my spiritual batteries. The museum offered exhibits on the history of evangelism and an inspirational area for prayer and meditation. This included the Rotunda of Witnesses.

The Rotunda was, uh, a rotunda – a large round room with a high domed ceiling. Nine twenty-foot tall banners encircled me. Done in silk, velvet and linen, the stunning banners depict Christian witnesses throughout the centuries and quote their pithiest sayings.

Oswald Chambers practically reached out from his banner and smacked my Inner Mess on the side of its putrid head. Chambers had served as a missionary and Bible teacher in the nineteenth century. The banner shows him sitting at a desk with an open Bible. His hands are folded and his head is bowed in prayer.

The top of the banner reads: 'If Jesus was only a teacher, then all he can do is to tantalize us by erecting a standard we cannot come anywhere near.'

'Right on!' my spirit concurred. The Christian life required a standard I could not come anywhere near. I was being tantalized. Two and half decades of spiritual tantalization! That's what I felt! That was my struggle. At last, somebody gets me! Oswald Chambers understood my problem.

The W.W.J.D. standard was not only hard, it was

impossible. Utterly, completely, totally, absurdly impossible. Maybe Jesus really meant it when he said, 'With men it is impossible.' My skin tingled. Something big was happening.

The foot of the banner completed Chambers' statement.

'But if we know him first as Savior by being born again from above, we know that he did not come to teach us only: he came to make us what he teaches we should be.'

'He came to make us what he teaches we should be.'

I was then in my twenties. This was that primitive era before P.D.A.s, cell-phone cameras, and the Internet. I grabbed some museum literature, borrowed a pencil from the receptionist, and wrote down the whole quote, around the edges of a brochure.

Jesus didn't come to tantalize me. He doesn't erect hurdles no human can jump. He doesn't pelt me with unreachable standards or shackle me with unbearable demands. He didn't travel all the way from heaven to earth to the cross, and back to heaven, so that I could fight a war of attrition with my Inner Mess. So why did he come?

'He came to make us what he teaches we should be.' Really? It's not I, but Christ? *He* makes me into that person he teaches I could be? That's what Chambers was saying, and that's what made my skin tingle.

Chambers dangled the key that unlocked my spirit from its Inner Mess prison.

Suddenly, W.W.J.D. took on new meaning for me.

What would Jesus do? Whatever it was, *only Jesus could do it*. Only Jesus could do what Jesus would do. Only Jesus could be a W.W.J.D. kind of person. His life represents a standard no one else could achieve. I knew that, but it had never really sunk in. Somehow, standing in the Rotunda of Witnesses, I finally got it.

If Jesus wasn't ready to relive his life in me and through me, Christianity was a charade. I felt like a kid in a toy store. I didn't know where to look next. A hooker pointed the way.

What Would Jesus Do? The Grace Edition

She paced outside the door, wondering what the men inside would do. What were they talking about? Business? Politics? Religion? She didn't care. She had to talk to a man in the room, but had no appointment. She agonized over the welcome she'd receive. She had seen the other men professionally and didn't fear them. But the one man she had never met was the only one she really wanted to see. For her, this meeting wasn't professional, it was personal. She opened the door and stepped inside.

Whispers and frowns greeted her. She ignored them. She found the man she sought.

> *A certain immoral woman heard he was there and brought a beautiful jar filled with expensive perfume. Then she knelt behind him at his feet, weeping. Her tears fell on his feet, and she wiped them off with her hair. Then she kept kissing his feet and putting perfume on them.*
>
> (Luke 7:37, 38, NLT)

What would Jesus do? The legalists dining with Jesus condemned her. They expected Jesus to do the same. Just as you probably expect Jesus to condemn the seedy characters on your bus.

We desperately need to turn around the W.W.J.D. question. Instead of asking What Would Jesus Do? with regard to *imitation*, we need first to ask it with regard to *transformation*. Here's what I mean.

What would Jesus do if he met a penitent hooker on the streets or at a party? Most Christians would say he would embrace and forgive her. Now, let's personalize the question.

What would Jesus do if he met your Inner Hooker? Or your Inner Thug, Inner Jerk, Inner Sinner, Inner Saint, or C.I.A. Agent? Inner Victim, Inner Martyr? Your Hypocrite? Your Liar? Your Legalist? Your whole shadowy zoo? What would Jesus do?

Smack them down? Preach a sermon? Condemn them? Blast them to hell? My hunch is that most Christians suspect that Jesus will rip off his 'love-the-sinner mask' and reveal the 'scary-executioner' identity he's been hiding all along.

That's what I always suspected. Now I know better.

Jesus is nothing like the Pharisees who condemned that immoral woman. He's the opposite. He's the un-Pharisee. They rejected her. Jesus accepted her.

> *'I tell you, her sins — and they are many — have been
> forgiven, so she has shown me much love. But a person
> who is forgiven little shows only little love.' Then Jesus
> said to the woman, 'Your sins are forgiven'.*

> (Luke 7:47, 48, NLT).

What would Jesus do if he climbed on board your bus and met every character lurking at the back? He would do for them what Harry Saulnier did for the down-and-outs at the Pacific Garden Mission. He would put his arm around each one. He would touch. Embrace. Comfort. Forgive. Transform. Set free. No matter how smelly, how diseased, how infested, or how decrepit. Not one character at the back of your bus has sunk too low for the love of Jesus. Jesus would love them.

That's what Jesus would do.

That is the central W.W.J.D. in Scripture. It is the opposite of what generations of underachieving Christians have been trained to believe. Sanctification has to be about *transformation* before it can ever be about *imitation*.

There is no character on your bus, no matter how nasty, that has gone past the point of redemption.

Oswald Chambers was spectacularly right. Jesus didn't come simply to teach us how to live. He came to make us into what he says we should be. He does it. It's his power. Therefore, it is all grace.

Four Shifts

Your Inner Mess feels about grace the way Gollum felt about Sauron's ring: a love/hate relationship. Love, because grace enables it to feel off the hook for its crimes. Hate, because grace spoils your Inner Mess's macabre party and turns you into a charity case before God.

But you have to get over your resistance to grace, because the only way to break free from Inner Mess domination is *to grace your Inner Mess*.

You can't beat it down, but you can disarm it through grace. How? By making four mental shifts.

From legalism to grace-orientation. Legalism reopens your father-wound and rubs it raw. It stimulates the flesh. It makes you feel worthless, guilty, arrogant or superior. It erects standards you can never achieve. Legalism convinces you that God doesn't love you and can't approve of you.

But he does love you. And through Christ, he does approve of you. Grace means that God always sees you through the lens of Jesus, and when you shift from legalism to grace-orientation, you'll see yourself that way too.

From shame to acceptance. Reality check: you *are* a blue-plate-special. You have an ingrown family of manipulative, victimy, crooked and sometimes dangerous, Inner Mess lurkers within. Yet you drown yourself in shame. The irony is that you accept others a dozen times a day in spite of their Inner Mess. Scripture commands such love. Why, then, will you not believe that God wants you to accept yourself in spite of your own Inner Mess? This does not excuse your Inner Mess; it just paves the way for real change.

From perfectionism to good-enough-ism. It's a safe bet that the more perfect someone's façade, the more lunacy lurks at the back of the bus. I hereby give you permission to be not perfect. Instead, it's good enough to be good enough. I officially set you free from the drive to be a perfect mother, father, pastor, son, daughter, or Christian. I wouldn't want you performing brain surgery on anybody, but wherever 'good enough' works as a philosophy, I say adopt it. Nowhere does the Bible call for you to be perfect, in spite of what your mother-in-law might say.

This does not justify your carnal tendencies and, if you use it that way, you'll reap what you sow. I just want you to see yourself as God sees you: as an imperfect person on a journey toward wholeness *who doesn't have to fake being perfect.*

From secrecy to confession. As John Ortberg writes, 'Everybody's normal until you get to know them.'[1] Most of us, out of fear of broadcasting our abnormalities, are content to remain unknown. Yet God insists that his people act like a body. That requires a handful of relationships in which you are fully known. A trusted friend, your small group, your pastor, a counselor. Someone. God is gracious, but he uses flesh-and-blood people as his hands to serve, arms to embrace, ears to listen, and hearts to love. When you let a trusted friend really see your nasty Inner Mess characters, suddenly grace moves from an abstract theory to hardwiring in your personality.

Your pick: legalism or grace. If Jesus were advising you, what would he say?

An External Power

Some time ago, a TV documentary showed a baby beluga whale grounded on a rocky beach. The tide had gone out and the poor whale was left to flop around on the shore while the sun rose in the sky. Too heavy to lift himself, the whale could only flop and tremble and squeak. The rocks cut into his delicate skin; a puddle of blood grew around him. Humans, including a film crew, gathered around. It was sad to see.

Meanwhile, the beluga's whale pod swam just a few yards away, listening to his pathetic squeaks and squeaking back to him. The whole scene was distressing.

That is how we are when we have no solution to our Inner Mess. We flop around, get nowhere, and wound our fragile selves in the process.

Finally, the tide came in. It gently lifted the baby whale to freedom and he rejoined his group.

This is grace. Another power comes in and lifts us to freedom. Another power reconnects us with God, ourselves, and those we love. We can never subdue the flesh on our own; it's impossible. Religion fails every time.

But God promised, 'For sin shall not have dominion over you, for you are not under law but under grace' (Romans 6:14). It's time to end sin's dominion – its right to rule our lives. It's time to depose the Inner Mess. Grace is the only power that can make it happen. Grace is the only power that makes the W.W.J.D. lifestyle achievable and even desirable.

But grace might not be what you think it is.

Taking Out the Trash

How would you rate your own W.W.J.D. track record?

In your opinion, how do most Christians approach a W.W.J.D. lifestyle? Do most Christians think it is achievable? If so, by what power?

Have you ever felt as if Jesus was tantalizing you with a standard you could never reach?

How confident do you feel that you have a *biblical* approach to achieving the W.W.J.D. lifestyle?

How does the concept of 'gracing your Inner Mess' sit with you?

What clues does Philippians 2:13 give about achieving the W.W.J.D. standard: 'For it is God who works in you both to will and to do for His good pleasure'?

Prayer: For your personal growth in grace and holiness for the glory of God.

Chapter 10

The Cross

'There is more mercy in Christ than sin in us.'
Richard Sibbes, 1577–1635

Scott's head throbbed; his heart pounded. A passenger had just robbed his bus; the unconscious body blocked the back exit. Another passenger – a cop – lay crumpled at the back with a bullet in him. Now the felon had a gun and was headed toward Katie. *Just when did I lose control?* The felon's gruff voice snapped him back to reality.

'You,' he said, looking at Katie, 'you're coming with me.' Blood streaked the felon's face and dripped from his scalp. Jason stood and shoved him hard with his shoulder, but the felon slammed the gun-butt down on Jason's head. He folded in half as the felon grabbed Katie's sleeve. She stopped resisting when he waved the gun at her. The felon yanked Katie into the aisle and headed for the back door.

Scott jumped up, blocking the way. The felon leveled the gun at Scott's chest. 'She's coming with me and you ain't gonna stop me.'

'No she's not,' said Scott. Then he spoke the words he was sure he'd regret for the rest of his life.

'Take me instead.'

'You? What do I want with you?'

Scott's mind raced for answers. 'Um, the cops are almost here. I'll be your shield. Just let her go. Take me instead.'

The felon licked his lips and looked at Katie. 'She'll be

my shield. Now move him.' He ordered Scott to move the punk's body out of the way. Scott hesitated. 'Don't be a hero. Just move him.'

Scott gulped. *Where are the cops? I gotta stall him…*

Scott stood his ground. 'I'm not moving him. Take me instead. Or you can shoot me. But I'm not letting you off this bus with her.'

The felon pointed the gun at Scott. 'I'll give you till three. One…'

Scott planted his feet in the felon's way and took his stand. Katie squeezed her eyes shut.

'Two…'

Oh, Jesus! What have I gotten myself into? God, watch my family. Watch my family. 'Take me. We'll walk off the bus. You can escape. I'll be your shield. Take me instead.'

The felon's head spun to the front of the bus as somebody else spoke with deadly calm: 'Three!'

* * *

> *For the message of the cross is foolishness to those who are perishing, but to us who are being saved it is the power of God (1 Corinthians 1:18).*

In the last chapter we unearthed the first piece of our Inner Mess puzzle: grace.

In this chapter we add yet another piece to the puzzle. I discovered this piece during my mother-of-all Aha! moments. It took me a long time, though, to understand how other pieces interlocked with it. I hope I can save you some time.

The Bleachers, the Flesh and the Cross

I found this piece of my Inner Mess puzzle while sitting in the bleachers of a large urban high-school gym. Actually, this piece found me.

I was never very good at physical education so I felt relieved one afternoon when my gym coach was absent. During those periods, our class sat in the gymnasium stands and read or did homework. I had brought along a book about Satan and decided to read it.[1] If I played my cards right, maybe I could blame the devil for all my Inner Mess woes. I was partly right.

The last part of the book suggested that the devil used guilt to manipulate Christians. I thought, *You've got that right.* The author compared guilt to a handle attached to my back. He said that Satan routinely grabbed the handle, slammed me around and sent me crawling back to my lukewarm life. I read, transfixed, sitting on the edge of those hard, wooden bleachers. *This author has been following me around.*

Sounds from a pick-up basketball game echoed in the gym. Some of my classmates studied, some chatted, and others dozed. I entered a zone. I devoured my book for a solution to my flesh-induced, lifelong guilt-trip. When I found my solution, it was not what I expected.

I expected the standard exhortation to pedal faster – and, believe me, my Inner Mess was perfectly poised to inflict even heavier demands on me. But I got none of that. I got the opposite.

By the time I had finished my little book in that cavernous school gym, I knew my pedaling days were over. I was even ready to trash the bike forever. What made the difference?

The first explanation of the death of Jesus that ever clicked with me. I had heard the story countless times. But this was the first time it had reached deep inside me and made sense. For the first time I understood both the logic and the love of Christ's death. I remember experiencing a cliché: I actually felt a burden roll off my shoulders. Having heard that phrase so many times, I was shocked to actually feel it.

Grace is Not Leniency
My wife, Margi, teaches Business Law at a Christian university.

She expects a lot from her students. During one class, after a tough exam early in the course, a handful of students pleaded for grace. They had given only half-hearted effort in their studies and had done poorly in the exam. They asked Margi to relax the grading curve so they could pass. 'Your husband teaches grace all the time,' they said. 'Show us grace.'

In her loving, lawyerly way, Margi shredded their pathetic logic. She pointed out the differences between grace and leniency and came home flabbergasted that Christian students could distort grace so easily. She also suggested that I'd best get busy clarifying exactly what grace does *not* mean.

So, in the name of marital harmony, and for all those passengers on your bus that would disfigure the grace of God, here goes.

Most people, including Christians, make a colossal theological error when they think of grace. They think it means that God was nice and relaxed his standards. Or that God loves them by overlooking their faults and embracing them anyway. Most people confuse grace with *leniency*.

Your Inner Mess relishes that idea the way a snotty-nosed brat relishes permissive parents. She gets to run amok in an arena of undefined boundaries and never face the consequences.

God's standards, however, are not arbitrary. They flow from his nature. God's standards – supremely embodied in the Ten Commandments – are God's standards because God's nature is God's nature. For God to relax his standards, he would have to alter his nature. Lions will become tofu-loving vegetarians before that happens. God cannot be lenient without ceasing to be God. Grace is not leniency, no matter how much our victimy whining wants to make it so.

If you've had your morning coffee, you must realize that no one in their right mind wants a God who is lenient. You don't want to live in a universe with a permissive, lenient God – a universe in which evil runs amok and the jerks of the world act with impunity. Think of all the death-row sadists who would simply walk away scot-free if there were no justice. Think of Hitler ordering babies to be tossed into ovens and a supreme deity being too wimpy to care. A universe with that kind of god would be nightmarish. An un-lenient God is the only way to go.

But that seems to land us in the middle of a dilemma. If God doesn't relax his standards, then how does he love the blue-plate special called *me*? I have a huge pile of maggot-ridden beef on my plate – how can an unyielding God accept a rancid dish like me? What's to keep me from cowering at the back of my bus for the rest of my existence, waiting for the hammer of God to fall?

In two monosyllables: The cross.

God has found a way to maintain his standards and love me anyway. That is why Jesus died and rose again. And, in a way you'd never expect, God made the cross of Christ the new Prime Directive for your Inner Mess. It is the foundational building block for any Inner Mess antidote. Judging by the flies buzzing around your Inner Mess, you need it, fast.

The Cross 101

Your Inner Dummy dreads theology like a non-flosser dreads the dentist's chair. So before you generate your own high-pitched squeal, let me encourage you. We'll break down the theology of the cross into two bite-sized pieces. Be forewarned – and don't blank out – when you read that both pieces have menacingly incomprehensible names: Imputation and Propitiation. I'll do my best to translate them into normal-speak.

Imputation: Who Picks Up the Bill?

The orange flame shot toward the ceiling as happy people around the table yelled, 'Opaa!' We had ordered *saganaki*, a melted cheese served hot and ignited tableside. One of my friends, Tony, speaks fluent Greek and knows Greek food. I rarely skipped an invitation to accompany him to our favorite Greek restaurant. One day I got more than great food, I also got a theology lesson.

After plates overflowing with *saganaki*, salads topped with *feta* and *gyros*, Tony asked for the check, in Greek. Something he said made my seminary-afflicted ears perk up. I don't speak Greek, but one word jumped out at me. Tony asked for *ton logariazmon* – 'the check, please.' I had heard that word before and didn't expect to hear it in a restaurant.

It's part of a family of financial terms in the Bible. While the exact word for 'the check' (*logariazmos*) isn't found in the Bible, its cousins are. The words refer to an accounting or to the reckoning of a debit or credit.

Paul uses a similar word: 'Blessed *is* the man to whom the LORD shall not impute (*logizomai*) sin' (Romans 4:8). How can God *not* impute sin to our accounts? God can't simply make my sins vanish; that would mean he lowered his standards. And that would land us right back in the lenient, nightmarish cosmos, which both logic and Scripture deny. If my sins are not imputed to my account, then who picked up the check?

Jesus did. When Jesus hung on the cross, God imputed our sins to him. All the sin of all humankind was credited to Christ's account. Actually it was a gigantic debit. He became the Lamb of God who 'takes away the sin of the world' (John 1:29).

You might have heard that Jesus died 'for your sins'. Have you ever thought about what that really means? It means he took delivery of each and every sin of yours and died for them. Jesus picked up your check as if he'd rung up the debt.

What can you say about that kind of love?

You can say only, 'Thank you.'

All my life, my Inner Mess had labored to atone for sins *that had been already imputed to Christ.*

No wonder God says he has cast our sins into the depth of the sea, put them behind his back, forgotten them and made us white as snow.[2] Not because he is lenient, but because he is righteous and has imputed them to Christ's account instead of ours.

Take that, Inner Saint, Inner Pharisee, Inner Judge! My

sins are gone. Christ himself took them to the cross. But what did he do with them?

Propitiation: Can I Actually Satisfy God?

A Sunday-school song haunted my teenage mind. It asked, 'But the question comes to me when I think of Calvary, is the Savior satisfied with me?'

My Inner Mess routinely answered, 'No way!' But everything changed during my big 'Aha!' moment sitting in those high-school bleachers.

QUESTION: What will it take for me to satisfy God?
ANSWER 1: More than I could ever do.
ANSWER 2: But not more than Jesus could do.

The Bible illustrates what Jesus did with my sins through a powerful ritual.[3] On the holiest day of their ancient calendar, the Day of Atonement, the Jews gathered to watch their theology dramatized. The high priest selected two goats. He laid his hands on the head of one goat while confessing the sins of the people. This symbolized that the people's sins were imputed to the goat, just as they would one day be imputed to Christ. That goat, called the 'scapegoat,' was led into the wilderness and sent away for good.

The high priest then sacrificed the second goat and caught its blood in a bucket. Next, he disappeared into the tabernacle, into its innermost chamber.

In that cramped tent-within-a-tent rested the Ark of the Covenant. The Ark was a wooden box overlaid with gold. The cover, or Mercy Seat, was solid gold. In Greek, the Mercy Seat was called *hilasterion* – the place of propitiation. Don't blank out on me now. We're just lighting the fireworks, and when we return to *hilasterion*, you'll let out a satisfied 'ooh' or maybe a highly blessed 'ahh.'

On each end of the Mercy Seat stood a solid gold angel. The two angels faced each other. Their wings were outstretched and their eyes looked down, as if peering into the Ark. The angels represent the holiness of God.

The Ark contained the tablets of stone with the Ten Commandments. Those stone tablets represent God's demands and humanity's failures.

Here's the symbolism so far: When God, in his holiness, looked down, he saw the Law, the ultimate symbol of God's demands and human failures. God could never be satisfied with that.

On the Day of the Atonement, the high priest carried the bucket of blood before the Ark and splattered it on the mercy seat – right in the sightline of the golden angels.

Now, instead of looking down on God's demands and humanity's failures, God's holiness looked down on the blood – the symbol of death and full payment for sin – and was *satisfied*. God's unrelenting demand for justice had been satisfied by the death of a substitute. Of course, a goat could never fully atone for humankind's sin, but it was a fine stand-in until the Lamb of God came to finish the job once for all.

But what does this have to do with me and my Inner Mess? you query. It's simple. Your Inner Mess thrives in the dank soil of an undervalued cross.

God punished Jesus for my sins instead of punishing me. That punishment was total. Whatever punishment my sins deserved, God meted out on Christ. Whatever condemnation, guilt, shame, judgment, wrath, or rejection – you name it – if my sins deserved it, Jesus Christ endured it. This is the core message of the cross.

And by enduring it, he *satisfied* the justice of God once for all for my sins. He did it all. I didn't help one bit. I didn't improve my moral batting average. I didn't eradicate my flesh or evict my Inner Mess. I didn't turn over a new leaf. I didn't do anything. I didn't give God anything. I couldn't; I didn't have anything to give. He did it all. God forgave me entirely on the basis of the cross. The only thing I contributed to the whole deal was my sin.

Fourteen centuries after Moses inaugurated the Day of Atonement, Jesus was nailed to the cross. Why? John wrote, 'In this is love, not that we loved God, but that He loved us and sent His Son *to be* the propitiation [*hilasmos*] for our sins' (1 John 4:10). He became the Mercy Seat incarnate. Christ satisfied God on my behalf, for once and for all. That's what hit me squarely in my young Italian-American face as I sat in that echo-filled gym.

Why was my Inner Mess making me work so hard to satisfy a heavenly Father who was already satisfied?

Ancient religions offered a completely different picture of propitiation. In those religions, emotionally fickle gods were pacified through countless sacrifices. But in biblical faith, God is never fickle. Propitiation does not pacify his emotions; it satisfies his justice.

Christ is the lightning rod that short-circuited the condemnation I had coming; he took the hit, fully and without reservation. There's nothing to add. There is no more price to pay. Jesus cried out, 'It is finished' and he meant it (John 19:30). In fact, another way of translating 'It is finished' is 'Paid in Full.' Jesus picked up the check and paid my debt. The bill is satisfied. The bill collector is satisfied. God is satisfied.

It seems as if everybody who needs to be satisfied is satisfied – except my Inner Mess.

Propitiation means that Christ paid in full every moral and legal debt you've rung up. You can list your most heinous crimes or sins – real and imagined, past, present, and future – and then stamp them all 'PAID IN FULL.'

Cruelty and abuse... PAID IN FULL
Religious intolerance and hypocrisy... PAID IN FULL
Hatred and murder... PAID IN FULL
Adultery and fornication... PAID IN FULL
Abortion... PAID IN FULL
Lying and treachery... PAID IN FULL
Pride and arrogance... PAID IN FULL

Crossing sexual boundaries… PAID IN FULL
Gossip and slander… PAID IN FULL
Inner Mess domination… PAID IN FULL
Every failure, sin, evil, and hypocrisy of my Inner Mess…
PAID IN FULL.[4]

I think my Inner Mess missed that memo. God is satisfied with me on account of Jesus Christ's death. That is real love.

When that reality hit me, I felt a burden roll away. My school gym became a sanctuary. I finally got it. So much that, now, when the question comes to me of whether my Savior is satisfied with me, the answer is crystal clear: *Yes he is, and on account of the cross, he always will be.*

God wants me to lean so heavily on the cross that the devil can't stick in a guilt-trip edgewise.

But you might think, *Tell me something I don't already know. I've heard a million times that Christ died for my sins. What I don't get is how that sets me free from a flesh-dominated life.*

That's because you're still missing union with Christ – a crucial piece of the Inner Mess puzzle. We'll get to it in the next chapter. But there's one question we've not yet answered.

Making it Personal

How do I make the cross personal instead of just theological? That is the question. If Jesus, by his cross, accomplished so much for me, how do I make it all mine?

The answer is so simple that most people reject it. Your Inner Mess will object: 'It's too good to be true. It's too easy. It makes us morally lax.'

The way to make Jesus personal is just to say *Yes*. God is offering you a gift. He's waiting for you to say 'Yes'. *Yes* to grace, the cross, forgiveness, acceptance, adoption, a new start in life. *Yes* to resting on the finished work of Christ. And, most of all, *yes* to Jesus.

Saying *yes* is another way of expressing to God that you have placed your faith in Jesus.

If that sounds too easy, it is only because Jesus did all the heavy lifting.

And if that sounds too uncomplicated, then spend some time unraveling this verse, and you'll come up with *just say yes*: 'God has appointed him as the means of propitiation, a propitiation accomplished by the shedding of his blood, to be received and made effective in ourselves by faith' (Romans 3:25, Phillips).[5]

That *yes* automatically entails a collection of *no's*. It's an exclusive *yes* to Jesus. That means you also say *no* to every other god, every other religion, every ritual, human performance, morality, good works and any confidence beside Jesus. You have to die to your self-confidence, self-effort, and self-promotion. *Yes* means faith alone in Christ alone.

I told you it was so simple that many people reject it.

I've had people get really angry when I explain this. They say, 'But I have to do *something*.' I answer, 'You can't. You're dead (Ephesians 2:1, 2). Dead people can't do anything, right?'

Or, 'I have to give God my life.' I say, 'You don't have a life. You're dead, remember?'

That makes them extra mad.

Then they say, 'I have to give God my heart.' I point out, 'It's a sewer; he doesn't want it' (Jeremiah 17:9).

That makes them feel really close to me.

The truth is glaringly simple: Jesus gave his life for you that he might give his life to you and live his life through you. He's the giver. You're the receiver. Don't reverse it.

And once you receive Jesus and his gift, he will board the bus and meet your Inner Mess. Every last decrepit character. What a day that will be! Correction: what a *beginning* of a new life that will be! He'll change you from the inside out, but not all at once. He'll make the W.W.J.D. lifestyle actually attainable by a power you never had before. As you grow in gratitude, you'll follow his steps and love him back.

Right now is an excellent time to say your *yes* to Jesus.

Don't let your Inner Mess hold you back. I had met Jesus for the first time as a little boy – the day of my salvation. I met him again in a cavernous high-school gym – the day of my assurance. He can meet you wherever you're at today.

The next time the devil reaches for the handle on your back and your Inner Saint reaches for the whip, tell them about the cross. And remind them that, on account of the cross, Jesus is faster at forgiving than you are at sinning.

Taking Out the Trash

··

Have you ever felt that the devil uses guilt like a handle on your back? How have your guilt and shame affected your relationships, schooling, and career?

How satisfied is God with you? Deep inside, do you really feel that your Father in heaven is truly satisfied with you?

How do the twin truths of Imputation and Propitiation affect your understanding of God? Of salvation? Of church?

Respond to this statement: 'Your Inner Mess thrives in the dank soil of an undervalued cross.' For more on how you can respond to the cross, visit the Inner Mess online community at www.innermess.com

Meditate on these verses, and reflect on the great price Jesus paid for your reconciliation to God: Matthew 27:1–66; Galatians 6:14; Colossians 2:13–15; Isaiah 53:1–12.

Prayer: That you would develop a cross-centered view of Jesus, yourself, and your Inner Mess.

Chapter 11
The Galvanized Life

*'By faith thou art so glued to Christ that of thee and him
there becomes, as it were, one person.'*

Martin Luther, 1483–1546[1]

'You're not taking her or anybody. Let her go and get off this
bus.'

Scott's eyes darted to a heavy-set woman standing at the
front of the bus. The first passenger on board that day, she'd
caught his attention for her bright brown eyes standing out
against a weathered face.

'There will be no more robbing. No more killing. No more
kidnapping.' She spoke with unbending authority.

Scott noticed the felon's eyes get narrow and his jaw
tighten. 'If you know what's good for you you'll shut up.'

'No,' she answered. 'If you know what's good for you,
you'll put down that gun and let that lady go, Alan Carter.'
Nobody moved except her. She plodded toward him on heavy
legs, holding his eyes in a steady gaze.

'I know who you are. I knew you when you were in diapers.
I know about that phony charge that sent you to prison. And
I know that you're better than this.' The felon relaxed his grip
on Katie. She pulled away and rushed to Jason. The felon let
her go. He looked confused.

'Who told you my name?' Scott watched as the woman
touched the felon's shoulder.

'Never mind that now. Give the driver your gun.' With her

149

head she motioned Scott to take his gun. Scott's palms grew sweaty. Again, the woman motioned Scott to take the gun.

The felon didn't move. Scott took a step toward him and then stopped.

'After I get off the bus. I'll give him the gun after I get off the bus.' The felon held the gun pointed at the floor in Scott's direction.

'All right. But these people have suffered enough. Go ahead. Get off the bus. But leave that gun with the driver. Just go.'

The felon made up his mind. He stepped over the fallen punk, waving the gun to keep the passengers in their seats. Scott stepped out of his way. The felon turned to climb the three steps down and out.

'Remember, Alan, God answers your mother's prayers.'

The felon hesitated and looked back.

'Now give the driver your gun.'

Scott inched toward the back exit half believing that the felon would give him the gun. Whatever power this woman held over him, it was working. It was working on Scott too. For the first time since hell broke loose, he felt hope.

The felon lowered the gun and held it toward Scott. Scott reached out to take it.

Scott's hope was shattered in a way no one saw coming.

* * *

Union with Christ

'Tommy, I'm giving you twenty-four hours to pay up. Got that?' Roger squeezed wide-eyed Tommy against the wall, his forearm crushing Tommy's neck.

'I got it. I got it.' Tommy wheezed. Roger cracked him on the side of his knee with a nightstick. 'Remember, twenty-four hours. Not a minute more.' He released the sobbing man, turned, and strutted out of the door to his still-running squad car.

Through most of the 1980s a powerful organized crime gang muscled its way around Chicago. A Chicago cop – we'll call him Roger – secretly held a second job on the side: he worked as a Mafia loan collector. He threatened, intimidated, and beat up gamblers who were late paying back loans to the mob. He gained a reputation for getting the job done. Brutally.

But the good times didn't last. Roger grew cocky with his bosses – not the best plan for a cop on the take. He fell out of favor with Frankie, the big boss. Worrying for his own neck, Roger set up an exit strategy. He began stealing Mafia records that documented organized crime activity. He embezzled enough money to set himself up for life and then turned state's witness. His testimony brought down the 'Calabrese Crew', one of the most notorious crime families in Chicago's history.

The U.S. Department of Justice immediately enrolled Roger in the Witness Protection Program. They erased his past. They gave him a new name, a new identity, and a new life in a new city. Roger was warned that he could never again go back to his old life. He could never again dine in his favorite restaurants or contact his old acquaintances. He was dead to that life.

The old Roger died and a new one was born.

God does something similar to you. Bible scholars call it union with Christ – an enrollment of sorts in the Heavenly Witness Protection Program. The Bible says, 'Therefore, if anyone *is* in Christ, he is a new creation; old things have passed away; behold, all things have become new' (2 Corinthians 5:17).

God so identifies you with Jesus that everything that is true of Jesus in his human nature before the Father becomes true of you, too.

So what does that do to your Inner Mess?

It makes it squirm. That's because your Inner Mess has met its Terminator.

The Terminator

Your Inner Mess is nothing but a usurper. Adam, by his disobedience, lost the scepter of his life to the bossiest, nastiest Inner Mess characters on your bus. That's what Paul means when he says that 'death reigned' and 'sin reigned' in you (Romans 5:14, 21). Death and sin, the forces of your flesh, became the ruling power in your life. Don't take this personally; it's true of the whole human race. Picture a high-chair tyrant throwing a tantrum and ruling the roost.

We've already suggested that if Jesus boarded your soul's bus, he would bring grace to each fallen character on it.

But that grace does more than embrace and comfort you in your brokenness.

Grace also terminates your Inner Mess's right to rule your life, once for all. Grace deposes your Inner Tyrant and installs a new ruler on the throne. You may be surprised at who it is. But that has to wait a little.

Just because you have Jesus on board it doesn't mean that you stop wanting anti-W.W.J.D. stuff. Jesus doesn't terminate your Inner Mess. He terminates its right to rule. It's a subtle distinction, but if you miss it you'll be confused. And you'll be depressed. This Inner Mess overthrow happens instantaneously at the moment you receive Jesus. Though it happens all at once, it's easier to understand as a three-step logical sequence.

Step One: Union with Christ

When Margi and I married, we endowed each other 'with all our earthly goods'. In the eyes of God and the state, we became one. Her debts and assets became mine and mine became hers. For the record, I married up. I have a ring on my finger and some joint credit cards to prove it. We will spend the rest of our lives transforming our *official* union into a *lifestyle* union.

God unites every believer with Jesus. The most common biblical phrase for this is simply 'in Christ' or 'in him'. You are so joined to Jesus that everything that is true about Jesus becomes true of you.

So what is true about Jesus? Is he accepted by God? Then so are you. Is he beloved of God? Then God loves you as much as he loves Jesus. Is Jesus an heir of God? Then, by virtue of union with Christ, you are a joint-heir with Jesus of the treasures of the cosmos – equal shares with him. If it's true of Jesus, it's true of you.

In Christ you have an all-new identity: you are a child of God, a citizen of a heavenly kingdom, and spiritual royalty. That's who you are. It's true about you whether you feel it or not and whether you act like it or not. You no longer derive your identity from your father-wound or your Inner Mess. From your salvation onward, you derive your identity from your union with Christ.

You share Christ's history, destiny, possessions, status and identity. It's real. And even in those wretched moments when you live beneath your dignity, your deepest self remains your identity in Christ.

What does that do to your Inner Mess?

It terminates its dominion, in only two more easy steps.

Step Two: Union with the Death of Christ

A principle running *throughout the New Testament is that death dissolves legal obligations.*[2] It's hard to collect a debt from a corpse. When Adam surrendered dominion of your soul to the flesh, he created a legal obligation. You became a 'debtor to the flesh' (Romans 8:12). No matter how hard you try to stifle your Inner Mess, it just won't shut up. 'We have rights!' its characters shout.

How will God dissolve that legal obligation?

Simple. He'll kill you, legally speaking.

Because there's another relevant principle running through Scripture: *Christ's death counts for you.* So on the day you receive Jesus, God photocopies the death certificate of Jesus Christ and puts a copy in your file. His death counts for you as if you yourself had died. When God joined you to Christ, the union was so complete it included being joined to his death.

The Scriptures say you 'died to sin' (Romans 6:2,3). And you 'have been crucified with Christ' (Galatians 2:20). Or, 'those *who are* Christ's have crucified the flesh with its passions and desires' (Galatians 5:24). It's not your death in view in these verses; it's Christ's death, which counts for you. Your pre-Christ identity is a goner.

And since death dissolves legal obligations you can give a gigantic raspberry to your Inner Mess. If it complains, tell it to sue you. You don't owe your Inner Mess the time of day. Its rights were terminated when the old you – you plus zero – was terminated.

It's not enough, however, to simply have Jesus' death on your record. You need more. And, thank God, you get more.

Step Three: Union with Christ's New Life

You also get a new life, just as Jesus did after he died. Union with Christ's death provided a death certificate for your file. Union with his resurrection provides a birth certificate. This makes Easter not only a festive holiday, but an indispensable part of the Christian message. His death is your death, and his life – his resurrection life and all its potential – is your life. It is your new birth, your new birthright.

And in this new birth, you are born with an authority you never had before.

I grew up with the faulty impression that Jesus wanted absolute mastery over my life – as if I were trading bondage to the 'cruel' flesh for bondage to 'extremely nice' Jesus. Either way I wasn't free.

I was also taught that the solution to my flesh was to 'annihilate my ego', a teaching that has more to do with Eastern mysticism than with Christianity. 'Self-life had to die so that Christ-life could be in control.' 'Yield your will to Christ's will.'

Like many Christians, I grew up with the idea that I had

to surrender complete control of my life to Jesus. Today I know better.

He doesn't want control of my life, complete or incomplete. He wants influence. And he wants a relationship. And he wants me to freely choose a path that honors him.

While I understand the intent of these teachings about Jesus taking control of our lives, they overstate the case and confuse dedicated Christians. Before your Inner Saint slams this book down with yet another charge of heresy, let me affirm the necessity of obedience to and willing service of Jesus Christ. I affirm the necessity of a yielded will. But how do we achieve it?

A hit song in 2005 described a young woman who was making a mess of her life until she prayed, 'Jesus, take the wheel.'

Have you ever considered the possibility that he doesn't want it?

Picture yourself, steering down the road of life with Jesus in the passenger's seat. If you took your hands off the wheel and said, 'Jesus, take the wheel,' what would Jesus do?

I think he would command, *Get your hands back on that wheel and steer! I put you there for a reason. Now use your head, follow your heart and drive. I'm here. Don't worry. I'm the navigator, but you're the driver. Now drive!*

QUESTION: Who exactly should sit on the throne of your life?

ANSWER: 'For if by the one man's offence death reigned through the one, much more those who receive abundance of grace and of the gift of righteousness will reign in life through the One, Jesus Christ' (Romans 5:17).

ANSWER CLARIFIED: You, exactly, should sit on the throne of your life. You, the one who has received the abundance of grace and the gift of [imputed, divine] righteousness 'will reign in life'. You sit on the throne of your own life. You reign. I'm not making it up. It says so right here in the Bible. The deepest you. The best you. The you that is joined to Christ. You reign. Not Jesus. You.

God wants strong-willed men and women at the wheel of their lives. You're in charge. Jesus will speak to you, influence you, and guide you. He'll navigate. But he will never commandeer your bus. He doesn't want to. This is the royalty for which you were created. You reign. So drive. You have far more authority and freedom in Christ than you would under any other lord, including yourself.

This is your new authority by virtue of union with Christ's life.

Your Inner Thug, Inner Brat, Inner Sinner and the rest of your grumpy characters have had their licenses revoked. You have every right to tell them to pipe down and take a seat.

But you still sin. You still suffer the father-wound. You still unleash your Inner Jerk at times. You still lust – sometimes irresistibly – for lots and lots of stuff that Jesus doesn't want. If Jesus terminated the dominion of your Inner Mess, then why is it still stinking up the joint?

The Galvanized Life

'His legs are moving! He is dead, but his legs still move!' said Luigi. His assistant rushed to see. He could scarcely believe his eyes. The lifeless legs before him moved as if alive.

In 1771, researcher Luigi Galvani accidentally touched dissected frog legs with an electric current. They twitched. Those first 'galvanized' frog legs revolutionized science's understanding of animal motion. Muscles contract in response to an electrical impulse. Without that impulse – an outside power applied to the muscle – a frog leg is just another pan-fried appetizer that tastes like chicken.

And without an outside power applied to your union with Christ, your spirituality is just another incarnation of a Pharisee's heart.

When Roger entered the witness protection program,

his legal status irrevocably changed. But none of that would matter unless his everyday life reflected his new identity. He absolutely had to live out his new identity or face the mob's vengeance. For Roger, living that new identity required sheer, unaided will power, motivated by fear. For a follower of Jesus, it's different.

Because your new identity in Christ comes with its own energy supply, motivated by love.

Christ In You

Christ himself moved into you with the power to make your new identity real. Union with Christ isn't just you living 'in Christ'. It's also Christ living in you.

This is the monumental mystery that Christianity offers the world. Jesus didn't just come to teach you or to offer you a moral example. He redeemed you and then moved into you. He's on your bus with a new power.

Paul testified to this power:

> *I have been crucified with Christ; it is no longer I who live, but Christ lives in me; and the life which I now live in the flesh I live by faith in the Son of God, who loved me and gave Himself for me (Galatians 2:20).*

His old identity, Paul plus zero, has been crucified: 'It is no longer I [alone] who live.'

His new identity, Paul plus Christ, now lives his post-salvation life: 'but Christ lives in me.'

Roger, the cop-turned-informant, had to force himself to live out his new identity. But you don't have to; you never could anyway. Christ is with you and the power that flowed through him now flows through you.

The Christian life is galvanized by the power of Christ. The Bible asks, 'Do you not know yourselves, that Jesus Christ is in you?' (2 Corinthians 13:5). Jesus said, 'I am the vine, you are the branches. He who abides in Me, and I in him, bears much fruit; for without Me you can do nothing' (John 15:5).

Why does Jesus indwell you? He indwells you in order to complete the process of sanctification.

A.B. Simpson, an old-time church leader, wrote, 'Sanctification does not come by our efforts, but it is made available to us as the purchase of His death upon the Cross. It is ours by the purchase of Jesus just as much as forgiveness is. You have as much right to be holy and sanctified as you have to be saved... Sanctification comes through the personal indwelling of Jesus.'[3]

Have you ever noticed a concrete walk with weeds growing through the cracks? God implants the life of Christ in you in the same way a gardener plants a seed. That seed is alive with its own power. That seed will, of its own accord, grow up (Mark 4:27, 28). You can't make it grow, but you can hinder its growth. In the same way, *Jesus Christ is constantly trying to express his own life and character through you.* You don't create his life – Jesus does that. But you can hinder the expression of his life through your resistance.

Here's what makes your Inner Mess characters really freak out: *when Jesus boarded the bus of your life, he didn't come with an off-switch.* You can either cooperate with him or fight him. It's your choice. If you cooperate, your sanctification will be increasingly evident.

If you fight him, you will crack like that concrete sidewalk. When followers of Jesus sin, we are contradicting our new identity and resisting the inward force of Jesus Christ. Who do you think will crack first – you or Jesus?

Much to your Inner Mess's chagrin, he won't go away, he won't give up, he won't shut down, and he won't take a nap. He'll galvanize all that is good in you and cut the power to all that is bad.

Jesus Christ abides in you, and the secret of power is that you abide in him – hang in there, we'll talk about what that means. He has all the power you'll ever need. You just have to learn how to let his power operate in you. That's where the second source of power comes in.

The Spirit In You

If you were to play any professional sport – football, basketball, soccer, rugby, bowling, take your pick – would you rather have a champion's *equipment* or a champion's *soul*?

My whole spiritual journey told the story of a man trying to wear the outward equipment of a Christian without ever developing the soul of Christ. Outfitting your Inner Mess in the accoutrements of Christianity is like dressing a gorilla in a tuxedo – entertaining but ludicrous. We need the heart of Christ if we're ever going to live like Christ.

And the heart of Jesus Christ depended on the Holy Spirit.

Christians believe that Jesus is fully divine and fully human. In his deity, he is as much God as the Father and the Spirit. In his humanity, he is human just as we are, except for sin. Jesus, possessing two natures in one person, is without parallel and without analogy.

So if we are going to walk in his amazing steps, we have to ask, *By what power did Jesus live his earthly life?* How did he love morons? Perform miracles? Cast out demons? Stay true to his horrific destiny? How did he teach with authority? How did he overcome temptation? Where did he get his power?

Most Christians assume that, since he was God, Jesus simply used his own divine powers. When faced with a confusing dilemma, he tapped into his own omniscience. When faced with an obnoxious enemy, he tapped into his own divine love. When faced with an insurmountable obstacle, he tapped into his own omnipotence. When faced with the devil's temptations, he tapped into his own divine holiness.

The typical Christian, therefore, views Jesus as a sort of 'humanity-plus'. As if Jesus didn't really face the limitations of finite humanity. He resembles Hercules or some kind of god–human hybrid more than us mere mortals.

If this were the case, then what kind of example would he be? Not a good one. We would have to dismiss his relevance for our lives today. 'Of course he resisted temptation – he's

God.' Or, 'Of course he loved his enemies – he's God.' The unspoken conclusion is that, if he is God (which he is), and lived his earthly life by his own divine powers, then how could anybody realistically expect me to follow him? His earthly life becomes irrelevant to the average mortal on the street, because, as average mortals, we do not possess the dual natures of humanity and deity.

Come on, admit it. You've thought that way, haven't you? Your Inner Mess is all too happy to dismiss the relevancy of Jesus as a genuine role model for your life. The fact of his deity becomes an excuse to lower the standards of holiness.

But what if Jesus didn't use his own divine powers as the Second Person of the Trinity? What if he didn't tap into his own omniscience, omnipotence, holiness, and love? What if he voluntarily restricted himself? And what if he limited himself to the same powers that any Christian could tap into?

If that were the case, then he immediately becomes a valid example for the child of God, and his life becomes eminently doable.

So the Scriptures affirm, 'he emptied himself' (Philippians 2:7, NASB). Of what did he empty himself? Not of his deity – he always was and always will be God. Instead, he emptied himself of the *use* of divine powers he always possessed. Voluntarily. By choice. Motivated by love.

I want to emphasize this, because the distinction is subtle, yet all-important. And your Inner Mess is working overtime right now to distort this truth. Jesus never laid aside his deity. He never ceased being God. That would be impossible. He was, and is eternally, true God, along with the Father and the Holy Spirit.

At the same time, when faced with human trials and tribulations, Jesus consistently chose to rely on a power other than his own.

So when he was tempted, he did not tap into his divine holiness. And when he was perplexed, he did not tap into his divine omniscience. And when he felt weak, he did not tap into his own omnipotence.

So where did he get his power?

> *The Spirit of the LORD is upon Me, Because He has
> anointed Me To preach the gospel to the poor; He has
> sent Me to heal the brokenhearted, To proclaim liberty to
> the captives And recovery of sight to the blind, To set at
> liberty those who are oppressed...*
>
> (Luke 4:18)

The Holy Spirit upheld and empowered the earthly life of Jesus Christ.

The Spirit empowered his birth (Matthew 1:18), his preaching (Luke 4:18), and his ministry (Luke 3:22). The Spirit guided him (Luke 4:1) and cast out demons through him (Matthew 12:28). The Spirit spoke God's words through Jesus (John 3:34), performed miracles through him (Luke 4:14), and even raised him from the dead (1 Peter 3:18).

From birth through death, all the way to his resurrection, the power that Jesus utilized was the power not of the Second Person of the Trinity but of the Third, the limitless power of the Holy Spirit.

And that exact same power is available to every follower of Jesus today.

Mind-blowing, isn't it? Jesus drew power from the Holy Spirit. So can you.

God promises, 'Walk in the Spirit, and you shall not fulfill the lust of the flesh' (Galatians 5:16).

You have Christ in you. You have the Holy Spirit in you. You have every potential for living a galvanized life.

By His Divine Power

God says, 'I am the Lord who sanctifies you' (Exodus 31:13), yet immediately the majority of Christians scurry like busy little beavers to sanctify themselves. The failure rate only spotlights the fallacy that we can ever, by our own effort, walk in the footsteps of Jesus.

'O wretched man that I am! Who will deliver me from this body of death?' (Romans 7:24). Who will stop my Inner Mess from trashing my outer world? Only Jesus by his Spirit.

A youth pastor, Corey, shared his most embarrassing moment while speaking at a church high-school retreat. When he was in college, Corey was in great shape – strong, muscular, a bodybuilder and a football player. He told how one day, at a pool party, he noticed a pretty young woman lying beside the pool. Corey wanted to meet her, so he flexed his muscles, jumped into the pool, swam around a bit, and worked his way to the edge of the pool nearest her.

He struck up a conversation. When she saw him, she smiled instantly. She kept on smiling at him, laughing at his jokes, and blushing. Inside, Corey congratulated himself for being so cool. Even better, his buddies were watching and he was proud of himself for striking up a conversation with this beautiful woman.

Finally, he asked for her phone number and she said yes. He had to get a pen, so he hopped out of the pool and strutted to his table, next to his amused friends.

When he got there his friends were laughing at him. When Corey found out why, he turned a few shades of red. He also realized why she had been laughing the whole time. Corey had a long string of snot plastered on his face that stretched from his nose, across his cheek, to his ear.

Maybe Corey wasn't as hot as he thought he was.

It's that way for so many Christians, too. They strut their stuff, but they're not as hot as they think they are. They think they're gold-medal spiritual athletes because they've spent a lifetime impressing their fellow churchified saints. God is not impressed.

They have the outfit of a Christian but a flesh-dominated heart.

All the while God has made perfect provision for a new life, a new identity, and a new power. He has built into you a never-failing resource to stop your Inner Mess from trashing your outer world. He has set you up for a life galvanized by the power of Jesus Christ through the Spirit.

The provision is already in place.

The only question is whether or not you have the faith to use it.

The answer is not as simple as it sounds.

Taking Out the Trash

....

Which inner reality defines you more: your Inner Mess or your union with Christ? How do you see yourself? Which one gives you more of your identity?

How do you react to the teaching that you, not Jesus, should be at the wheel of your life? How does that fit with previous teaching you have received?

Have you ever dismissed Jesus' life as a relevant role model for your life because, 'After all, he's God, and we can't reasonably be expected to live like him'? How does that position contradict the biblical teaching of Jesus as not only true God, but also true human?

Has your Christian life depended more on your own power or on the Holy Spirit's power? Can you tell the difference?

What does Jesus suggest about the Galvanized Life in this verse? 'I am the vine, you *are* the branches. He who abides in Me, and I in him, bears much fruit; for without Me you can do nothing' (John 15:5.).

Prayer: That Jesus Christ might increasingly express his life and character through you.

Chapter 12

Faith

Habitual lively faith in Christ's presence and readiness to help is the secret of the Christian soldier fighting successfully.

J.C. Ryle, 1816–1900

'You ain't going no place, mister. Now do what the lady says and give him your gun.' All eyes turned to the hooker. She had picked up the fallen cop's gun and held steady aim at the felon's chest.

Scott froze. The felon turned his head slowly to face the hooker.

'Honey, put your gun down and let him go.' The heavyset woman plodded toward the back of the bus.

'After what he just did? I hate men like him. He ain't goin' nowhere.'

'Honey, just listen to me and put the gun down. I know it's hard, but you have to trust me.'

Seconds dragged by. Scott considered his options. He was close enough to grab the felon's gun. But that might mean another stray shot. Too risky. He couldn't reach the hooker fast enough. He could only wait. But something about that mystery woman gave him confidence.

'Trust me,' the woman told the hooker. 'Let him go.' The woman stopped just behind Scott. She exuded a courage he had never encountered before.

Scott took confidence from her. Almost before he could think, he spoke.

'Listen to what she says. Put the gun down and let this guy go.' He stepped around the felon, shielding him with his own body. He felt as if he were a detached observer. Logic told him he should be terrified, but he wasn't. He felt calm inside. *I sure hope this works,* he told himself.

He'd find out soon enough.

* * *

Danger

Just trust, I told myself. *You won't die.* My heart raced. My palms sweated. I argued with my fears. *You'll live through this. Just take the step.* I balked. My head told my legs to move, but so far they weren't listening.

Colorado's Royal Gorge is one of the most impressive tourist traps I've ever fallen for. The Royal Gorge is a thousand-foot-deep chasm with a raging river cutting through the bottom. Jagged rocks. Steep cliffs. A crack opened, no doubt, to hell itself.

Engineers have strung a rickety bridge over the chasm, suspended by wires. So maybe it's not all that rickety, and maybe it can bear the weight of the cars that cross it, but to an acrophobic like me, the so-called bridge might as well be suspended by twine.

The bridge sways back and forth violently – at least one or two whole inches in a strong wind. The bridge deck consists of heavy wood planks. My alarmed mind calculated that, for maximum survival possibilities, I should never put all my weight on a single plank. To heighten my dread, the planks are spaced about two inches apart, allowing an unwary pedestrian to see between them to the deadly abyss below. No doubt a trick by lawyers to absolve the owners of responsibility should I plummet to my demise. 'Your Honor, the deceased unquestionably saw the peril – we spaced the planks two whole inches apart – assumption of risk and all that.'

To top off their macabre mind game, the bridge designers constructed side railings out of a web of pencil-thin metal cables. I'll grant that this allowed unobstructed views of nature's beauty. But it also invited a scarcely hindered fall to one's death. Never mind the dozens of children prancing gleefully beside them and peering fearlessly through them. What monstrous parents they have!

For ten dollars you can walk a quarter mile across the Royal Gorge and back.

No refunds.

My Inner Coward hissed, 'Slink back to your car, scaredy cat!' My legs wobbled their agreement. But my Inner Cheapskate won the day. 'You paid your ten bucks and you're not leaving until you walk across this bridge.'

I perched for a moment at the edge to observe hundreds of imprudent tourists mindlessly flirt with death. *They're doing it*, I told myself. I located, as best as I could, the centerline. This would minimize my odds of being sucked over the edge.

With a sigh of finality and a rigid posture, I stepped onto the bridge.

In that moment, my belief transmogrified from what preachers call 'head knowledge' into 'heart knowledge'. It lived up to the Bible's standard of faith.

This faith is the missing piece in most Christians' Inner Mess puzzle. It is also the hardest piece of all to put into place.

The Faith that Sets You Free

Likewise you also, reckon yourselves to be dead indeed to sin, but alive to God in Christ Jesus our Lord.

(Romans 6:11).

You argue, 'I have plenty of faith, yet my Inner Mess still tyrannizes me.' Others might argue that faith is passive, yet gaining victory over the flesh is anything but passive. Let's get clear on the kind of faith that breaks us free from Inner Mess domination. It is a muscular, yielded, mature faith.

A Muscular Faith

Peter, again proving that his Inner Editor languished far away on a deserted island, blurted out, 'Command me to come to you on the water' (Matthew 14:28). Blustery winds, choppy seas, moonless night, no flashlights. My faith crossing the Royal Gorge overcame my fears. Peter's faith overcame physics. Peter, you win. What did it feel like to step out of that boat?

His friends look at him as if he's crazy. Peter hitches up his cloak. One leg goes overboard. His foot touches the icy waters. To his amazement, the water pushes back. He tests it; it holds his weight. Peter lifts out his other leg and plants his second foot on *aqua firma.* Imagine the rise and fall of the waves, the howling winds. Worse than the first time riding a bike. But he did it. Peter walked on water.

Was that faith? Yes. Was it passive? No. The other disciples were passive. They sat in their boat like armchair sportscasters analyzing Peter's game. They could analyze it theologically, psychologically and scientifically. They could discuss, debate, be in awe, live to tell the story, and stay dry. But they could never say that they walked on water. That privilege belongs forever to the only man who exercised a muscular faith in the power of Jesus to overcome the forces that limited his life.

If Jesus, through the Spirit, has enough power to walk on water, doesn't he have enough power to free you from your Inner Mess?

When I say muscular faith, I mean the kind of faith required to wrestle down all those instincts that make you doubt God. You exhibit muscular faith every time you act boldly in spite of self-protective resistance from your Inner Mess.

What would Peter's Inner Mess say about walking on water?

Inner Coward: Don't do it, you'll die!
Inner Liar: Don't do it but say you did.
Inner Legalist: You're not worthy.
Inner Skeptic: He's not able.

Yet Peter elbowed his way past those nay-saying, back-of-the-bus passengers and stepped out of the boat.

As Peter's story continued, the boisterous winds and the heavy seas distracted him. His faith wavered. He sank, and Jesus rescued him. At this point, I would expect a pat on the back for making it this far. High commendation and a medal of honor. But Jesus rebuked him. 'O you of little faith, why did you doubt?' (Matthew 14:31). Ouch! What can we conclude about Jesus' expectations for your faith?

They're higher than you think they are.

Jesus expects you to show the faith that walks on water, moves mountains, multiplies fishes, and raises the dead. Anything less merits scolding as 'little faith'. Not because Jesus is unkind but because he's realistic.

Do you believe that Jesus, through the Holy Spirit, can stop your Inner Mess from trashing your outer world? Can he make your marriage healthy and your family whole? Can he free you from enslavement to your father-wound? Is he able to break the power of your addictions? Can he dethrone the crazy parts of you and enthrone your noble self?

If you don't believe all that, you might as well hand your bus keys to your Inner Mess right now.

The only way to achieve victory over the flesh is by faith. Reckon yourself dead to sin and alive to God. Step onto the bridge.

But how fair is that? For every disciple who walks on water, a million sink, even with the most sincere faith. How can Jesus expect Peter-like faith, when, in the story of our lives, he has disappointed that faith so many times?

A Yielded Faith

American baseball fans in 1988 witnessed two extraordinarily opposite examples of pitching success and Christian faith. Two league-leading pitchers, both outspoken Christians, made headlines that year.

Orel Hershiser pitched his L.A. Dodgers to a World Series Championship, earning the league's Most Valuable Player award. On a late-night talk show, Johnny Carson asked Hershiser why, just before his final pitch to win the World Series, he paused and looked up for a few moments. Hershiser said he was singing his favorite song. Carson asked, 'Would you sing it for us?'

The request caught Hershiser by surprise – he blushed and said, 'Okay.' He then lifted his head and sang – to a national audience:

> *Praise God from whom all blessings flow.*
> *Praise Him, all creatures here below.*
> *Praise Him above, ye heavenly host.*
> *Praise Father, Son, and Holy Ghost.*

He even sang the 'Amen.' The studio audience erupted in cheers and Johnny Carson smiled broadly. A man of faith achieved the pinnacle of success and glorified God in the process.

Shift scenes to a second pitcher. In 1987, the year before Hershiser won the World Series, Dave Dravecky helped bring the San Francisco Giants to the World Series. They didn't win that year, but Dravecky's pitching brought them that far. Shortly after the World Series, Dave Dravecky was diagnosed with cancer in his pitching arm. He asked his fans to pray for God's healing. Dravecky underwent surgery in 1988 to remove half his deltoid (shoulder) muscle. A special procedure froze the humerus bone, hoping to eradicate any remaining cancer.

By the next season, Dravecky was pitching again in the minor leagues. Not long after this, he made a highly publicized major-league comeback, pitching a winning game against the Cincinnati Reds. Dravecky was hailed as a survivor and a hero. Another man of faith achieved the pinnacle of success and gave God the glory. But a clock was ticking and nobody knew it.

In the second game after his comeback, Dravecky had pitched three innings when he felt a tingling sensation in his arm. Two innings later, in a riveting moment replayed countless times around the world, Dravecky's career came to a crashing halt.

He stood on the mound, wound up, and threw the ball. Midway through the pitch, his forearm literally snapped in half with a sickeningly loud crack. Stunned fans watched in horror as Dave Dravecky − conquering hero and pillar of faith − dropped to the ground and writhed in agony.

The cancer had returned. Dravecky ultimately lost his entire arm, but amazingly never lost his faith.

Two top-tier athletes, playing the same position in the same sport with the same faith in the same God. Yet two completely opposite outcomes. So answer this question: *Did God reward Hershiser's faith but disappoint Dravecky's?* In those devastating moments when your faith goes unrewarded, what is going on?

God is teaching you that true faith leaves the outcomes to God. That's what I mean by a *yielded* faith.

Your job is faith; God's job is outcomes. He is the sovereign Lord of your life and your world. He has purposes in mind that you have no clue about. That's why you are to act in faith and yield the outcomes to him.

You can't control other people's reactions. You can't control the financial markets. You can't control your wife, husband, boss or kids. You can't control viruses or cancer cells or weather. You are not in control. God is.

Orel Hershiser could have turned arrogant. Dave

Dravecky could have turned bitter. Yet both men stayed faithful to God. They exhibited a yielded faith – yielded to the will of a Heavenly Father Who Knows What He's Doing. You need the same faith if you ever hope to stop your Inner Mess from trashing your outer world.

Sometimes you bask in victory. Other times the cancer returns, the child strays, the marriage collapses, the money disappears. Whether you sink or swim or walk on water, it is not the outcome *per se* that pleases God. It is your shining moment of faith – that's what pleases God. Regardless of the outcomes, it is your faith that wins the applause of angels, stockpiles treasures in heaven, and brings a smile to your Father's face.

Most importantly, it is faith that activates the power of Christ to overcome your Inner Mess. God has never once disappointed anyone's faith.

Job, like Dave Dravecky, suffered gut-wrenching loss. Even Job's own wife told him to curse God and die. Yet there – lying in ashes, scraping his oozing sores with broken pottery, feeling the sting of bankruptcy, grieving his children's deaths, and enduring the asinine philosophizing of his 'friends' – Job declared, 'Though he slay me, yet will I trust him' (Job 13:15).

With all that agonizing loss you would have expected a riot to break out on his bus. Instead we just see a quiet confidence, yielded to the will of God. Did he wrestle with doubts and questions and heartache? Most certainly. But his Inner Mess never took control. What was Job's secret? What exactly does it take to keep your Inner Mess from trashing your outer world?

It takes a Spirit-induced, muscular faith in the indwelling Christ – a faith that yields to whatever outcomes God deems fit. Only that faith can set you free from being dominated by your Inner Mess.

How can you develop it?

Faith

A Mature Faith

Faith is a choice. Sort of, but not exactly. Let me illustrate.

A while ago, I set up a weight bench on the stage in my church, and loaded a bar with 225 pounds. I asked my friend, Jason – a weight lifter – to help make a point during a sermon.

As I preached, I asked the church if lifting weights was a choice. They answered yes. Then I asked if bench-pressing 225 pounds was a choice. They hesitated. Jason came up on the stage, bench-pressed the weight a few times, and returned to his seat to thunderous applause.

Most of the audience, including me, couldn't lift that weight. Yet lifting weights is a choice, right?

It turns out not to be that simple. Jason had to work his way up to pressing 225 pounds. It showed in his physique. That's when lifting that weight became a *feasible* choice for him.

Faith is a choice in exactly the same sense. You have to work your way up to a consistently strong faith. That's what I mean by a mature faith. What are the odds that you'll lead with faith instead of your flesh in your next nightmarish ordeal? Those odds depend on your maturity.

I've observed all kinds of Christians over my thirty years in pastoral ministry and, in my observation, one obstacle blocks their progress more than any other: *intermittent motivation.* Christians who toggle on and off, on and off with God, prayer, Scripture, and the church. They never build up the momentum it takes to consistently triumph over the flesh.

So you're on fire for God – building spiritual muscle – for six months or six years, but then God doesn't answer a particular prayer. So you ignore him for a year. Your muscles atrophy. Then you feel needy or guilty and come back to God, determined to try harder. You return with a bang and a tearful testimony of repentance. You leap into church life and play guitar in worship and pray with energy. You start building muscle again – your faith grows stronger and steadier month by month.

173

Then some church lady convenes an Inquisition on the appropriate volume for an electric guitar. In disgust, you disappear for a couple of years. Again, your spiritual muscles atrophy. Until you have your first child. Then it's back to church.

This cycle of starts and stops stymies your spiritual growth and locks you in spiritual kindergarten. You keep starting over, rebuilding the same foundation, and never building a satisfying lifestyle on top of it. Your spiritual muscles grow and shrink and grow and shrink, as do the odds that you'll exercise a yielded faith in time of temptation.

In your spiritual phases, your Inner Mess plays along. Your Inner Saint enjoys the challenge of out-Christianing the next Christian. Yet, as Jesus warned, you honor God with your lips, but your heart – your bus and its passengers – is far from him (Mark 7:6).

In your 'I'm ticked off at God' phases, your Inner Mess churns out self-justification, self-pity, and self-absorption.

You need a mature faith. That requires a long obedience in the same direction.[1]

I'm frequently asked, 'Can a Christian live a sinless life?' Theologians don't agree. I don't believe in perfectionism – the idea that God eradicates your flesh in a special encounter some time after salvation. That's because when the writers of Scripture tell us not to sin, in the next breath they point to God's provision for when we do sin (1 John 2:1). They must not have believed in perfectionism either.

Does that mean that a sinless life is out of reach?

Hold that question and answer this one instead: Is it possible for you to go the next minute without sinning? And don't get hyper-spiritual and tell me that with every breath you draw you're a miserable sinner. I mean, in a *behavioral* sense, can you go one minute without sinning? Give it a try, I'll wait.

Answer? Yes. Well, if it's possible to go one minute without sinning, can you string two minutes together? Of course. How about an hour? Two hours? All morning?

When we ask if we can live a sinless *life*, we're missing the point. We should ask if we can live a sinless *minute*. If we can't, then God is powerless to change our lives. If we can, then we should string a bunch of those minutes together. You live in a succession of seconds and minutes and hours and days. Don't worry about your whole life. Worry about the next hour. Because in that next hour, by the power of God, you can live without sin. It's a choice you make.

But it's a choice that you must strengthen, too. You gain strength over time by means of spiritual growth. Especially by means of saturating your heart with Scripture (Romans 10:17; John 17:17). Growing deep with Jesus and his word doesn't make you perfect, but it does increase the odds that you'll exercise a muscular faith the next time you're tempted. You need to grow a faith that walks in the Spirit, draws on the power of Christ to overcome temptation, and welcomes Christ's power to either transform or disarm your incorrigible Inner Mess goblins.

You build this kind of faith in the same way that you build your muscles: incrementally and with lots of sweat. You need a spiritual workout regimen: Scripture, prayer, community/ fellowship, service, worship. And you need to stick with it, because the moment you stop, your faith shrinks.

Had Peter built up a more mature faith, who knows how far he could have walked on the water? Maybe he could have danced on the water. Or performed a tumbling run, ending with a back flip onto the boat, sticking a perfect landing.

Why do you think a consistent devotional life is so difficult? Your Inner Mess dreads its own ouster. So it clamors against time in the word, time in prayer, time in community with fellow Christians, and time serving others in the name of Jesus. Your flesh mobilizes against your spiritual growth. It blanks you out, distracts you, and puts you to sleep if it can. It will accept anything but a devotional life that signals the end of its reign.

The Struggle

A holy life is a mighty struggle. There is no room for passivity or laziness. But it is not the struggle you think it is. It is not a struggle directly against sin, or against the flesh, or against evil. It is not a struggle to imitate Christ directly, or do good works, or produce holiness, or subdue passions. If you're still pedaling up any of those hills, you can stop when your thighs start burning. I hereby set you free from all those futile exertions.

The real struggle is the struggle to *believe*. Fight the fight of *faith*. As often as you win that battle, all other victories fall into place.

Quit struggling against bad habits. Quit struggling to lose weight. Quit struggling to be more like Jesus.

Instead, fight tooth and nail to believe that what God has said is true, enough to act like it. Fight to believe that Christ in you has all the power you need to overcome temptation and addiction and evil.

But doesn't the Bible teach us to resist the devil that he might flee from us (James 4:7)? Yes, but it also tells us how: 'Resist him, firm in your faith' (1 Peter 5:9).

Doesn't the Bible tell us to strive against sin (Hebrews 12:4)? It does, but notice the context: we first fix our eyes on Jesus – a metaphor for faith – or the striving is in vain (verses 2, 3).

The fight is a fight of faith. The struggle is a struggle to believe in Jesus and to trust in the power of the Spirit. All other struggles are doomed to failure without faith first.

Faith is the victory. 'Fight the good fight of faith,' exhorted Paul (1 Timothy 6:12). He urged faith as our operational top priority: 'Above all, [take] the shield of faith with which you will be able to quench all the fiery darts of the wicked one' (Ephesians 6:16).

Faith puts you in the driver's seat and it makes your Inner Mess shut up and go for the ride. Faith puts you in full possession of your faculties. It activates the power of Christ, responds to his Lordship, and puts you in fellowship with the Spirit.

Exercise that muscular, yielded, mature faith, no matter how you feel. No matter what the outcomes. No matter what evidence to the contrary you may face.

I not only walked across the Royal Gorge and back, I even commanded my legs to wobble to the edge so I could peek down. Guess what! Jesus kept me from being sucked through the ridiculously thin side rails.

Victory.

Taking Out the Trash

Describe an experience in which you walked across a rickety bridge or made yourself do something scary. What lessons about faith did you learn?

How muscular is your faith? How yielded is your faith? How mature is your faith?

The teaching that you can be holy through faith in Jesus has been criticized as advocating passivity. Does the kind of faith described in this chapter sound passive to you? Why or why not?

What does Paul teach about the role of faith in Galatians 2:20: 'I have been crucified with Christ; it is no longer I who live, but Christ lives in me; and the life which I now live in the flesh I live by faith in the Son of God, who loved me and gave Himself for me' (Galatians 2:20)?

Do you believe that Christ in you is stronger than your Inner Mess? Do you believe that the Holy Spirit is stronger than your Inner Mess? Do you believe it enough to act like it – to step out in faith as if it were true?

Prayer: For a muscular, yielded, maturing faith in Jesus to release you from Inner Mess dominance.

Chapter 13

Community

'He said, 'Follow me and I will make you' — and there
are no self-made Christians in his service; they are all
Christ-made.'

Herbert W. Lockyer, 1988[1]

The hooker's body shuddered as she suppressed her anger.
'He ain't leaving.'

Scott stood his ground, shielding the felon with his own
body. 'Don't do this. Please. Put the gun down.'

Scott felt the heavyset woman touch his shoulder. She
moved beside him, joining the felon's human shield. 'Do what
he says,' she added. 'It's over.'

'You're letting him walk away? After what he just pulled?
No! It's payback time.' The hooker steadied the gun at Scott.
'Get out of the way.'

Scott closed his eyes. He breathed a prayer for his family
and said, 'I'm not moving.' The heavyset lady planted her feet
and said, 'Neither am I.'

The tract lady joined the group. 'I'm not moving either.
Let him go.'

Katie spoke. 'They're right. He doesn't belong here.'

Scott's head hurt and his heart pounded. The sirens still
sounded far away. Traffic started moving; someone behind
him laid on the horn.

'Let him go,' Scott said.

The hooker lowered her arm slightly. 'But it's not fair.'

'You're right,' said Scott. 'It's not fair, but so what? End
this now.'

The tract lady nodded her approval. Jason said, 'Yeah. There's plenty of blame to go around today. Let him go.'

'I don't know...' the hooker said. She lowered her weapon slightly.

Scott held his breath.

All heads turned when the felon snorted and spoke.

* * *

Secret Shame

Sweat beaded on Jeff's forehead and he couldn't look me in the eye. Jeff had grown up attending church and had just started attending mine. Now in his late twenties, he'd made an appointment for pastoral advice. He was an average-looking guy with a medium build and sandy-colored hair. He had dated a lot of women, and usually broke it up before the relationship got too serious. He sat in my office struggling to speak.

'Whenever you're ready,' I said.

Jeff couldn't seem to get the words out. His Inner Dummy had him bound and gagged.

'I'm doing something I'm not proud of,' he blurted out. 'And I can't stop.'

I looked at him and waited. He looked away. We waited some more.

Stuttering and stammering, Jeff revealed his anguish. He had planned to abstain from sex until he was married, but, in a moment of weakness, had hired a prostitute. His first sexual encounter was with a stranger, and now he felt miserable.

Jeff fell silent. He looked nauseous. He hazarded an agonized glance in my direction and quickly looked down.

At that moment, Jeff didn't need any added guilt, shame, or rebuke. He was doing a fine job at each of those himself. The Holy Spirit held him under heavy conviction. He didn't need me to add to that weight.

As I saw it, Jeff had two great needs: intercessory prayer and incarnated grace. He needed to obey James 5:16: 'Confess your trespasses to one another, and pray for one another, that you may be healed. The effective, fervent prayer of a righteous man avails much.'

Intercessory Prayer

I scoured the room for an escape as two heavily tattooed, profusely pierced bikers made a beeline toward me. A braided ponytail bounced behind the patch-laden, leather-vest-clad male of the duo; a black leather cap and fingerless gloves matched the leather chaps of the female. *This can't be good,* I told myself. *Run!* But it was too late.

The gigantic church was too crowded for a fast getaway. And the pastor had just decreed every first-time visitor's nightmare: he had told us to gather in clusters of three to pray for one another. What looked like two charter members of the Hell's Angels decided that I would be their third.

Lord, can't I visit a church in humble anonymity? Can't I just fade into the background? Must I always be serving others? Do I have some kind of mark that makes needy people – like these biker-dudes-from-hell – seek me out? Why, God? My Inner Whiner shifted into overdrive.

All right, Lord, I'll pray for these clearly anguished people, but I don't have to like it.

I faked a smile as the bikers greeted me. I opened my mouth to ask how I could pray for them, but they beat me to it. Each biker laid a gentle hand on my shoulder and lovingly welcomed me. They asked who I was and where I was from 'I'm Bill, from Chicago.' 'Oh! That's great! Bill, how can we pray for you?'

My resistance melted away as I realized that I, an exalted pastor of Almighty God and a doctoral student in divinity, was about to receive warm-hearted ministry from an unlikely pair of weathered California biker-dudes.

I needed it, because I carried a secret need that I hadn't shared with anybody but my doctor. I don't want to gross you out, but for this story to make sense, you need to know that my secret involved a persistent bloody discharge, every day for the past several weeks.

My new best friends repeated, 'Hey man, like, how can we pray for you?'

I plunged ahead. 'Well, for the last few weeks every time I've gone to the bathroom there's been a lot of blood and the doctors don't know what it is, and it scares me.'

Can you understand why I wouldn't put that prayer request in my church bulletin? I had visited doctors and I had prayed for my own healing, but so far nothing had worked. Just lots of bright-red blood and what looked like tissue paper mixed in. I hadn't told anybody. Every trip to the loo, without exception.

'Wow, Bill. Like, that would be truly scary. We'll pray for you.' With their hands on my shoulders, we got down to business.

The voices of a thousand people, clustered in triplets, echoed through the vast sanctuary like a waterfall, but all I heard were two biker-angels quietly urging God to heal me. When they finished I offered a perfunctory prayer for each of them, we embraced, and the worship service continued. No fanfare. No faith healers. No overt displays of divine power. Just a humble prayer.

I was permanently healed that day. I had prayed unsuccessfully for that healing for weeks. Too embarrassed to seek out other people's prayers, I'd kept it a secret and pleaded directly with God and with doctors. But my biker friends taught me a life-changing lesson.

God insists that his people act like a body. There are certain needs in every life that God will not meet until we ask other people to pray for us. 'And the eye cannot say to the hand, "I have no need of you"; nor again the head to the feet, "I have no need of you"' (1 Corinthians 12:21). To pretend self-sufficiency is to deny the very nature of the church. Authentic community is not optional for a growing Christian.

I, like my friend Jeff, desperately needed not just my own prayer, but intercessory prayer – the prayers of other people on my behalf. That meant I had to tell somebody. You too. So if God has not yet delivered you from deep-rooted Inner Mess patterns, even after you have prayed for deliverance, he could very well be waiting for you to fulfill James 5:16.

It isn't easy, and your Inner Mess hates it. It will resist you every step of the way. You have to show somebody the rotten spinach on your plate. Then you have to let them serve you while you stand by, watching them labor in prayer for you. The whole process is mightily humbling, so let me give you some pointers to make it easier.

Limit the number. Telling *somebody* doesn't mean blabbing to *everybody*. Find one or two people, or perhaps a highly focused small group. Have an explicit talk about confidentiality, but know that you're still taking a risk. Some churches offer anonymous prayer teams after their worship services. Whoever it may be, when you plunge into the icy waters of Inner Mess exposure – with non-judgmental people – you'll immediately feel release.

Use discretion in marriage. God designed marriage for your joy and for your healing. The more truthfully you can live with your spouse, the stronger your bond. Sometimes, however, confession may be good for the soul, but can be bad for your marriage. Think long and hard before you unburden your soul to your spouse. You might feel better, but your spouse is burdened with your pain and guilt, especially if you have sinned against him or her. We are to speak the truth *in love*, even in confession. Some truths – 'I really hated that stew you cooked last night' or 'That dress makes you look fat' or 'You're not wearing *that*, are you?' – are plain unloving, and you shouldn't state them. Regardless of your marriage's transparency level, you should still cultivate a spiritually mature, same-sex, trusted friendship outside your marriage, in which you can work through your struggles without constantly dumping your Inner Mess on your spouse.

Cultivate relationships. The kind of friends you can be transparent with will not find you. That means you have to cultivate relationships in order to find them. Most churches offer small groups, accountability groups, classes, or mentoring partnerships. Get involved. Volunteer for ministry. Join a summer mission trip. Keep trying until you find a friend or group that you can trust. Give it time. Don't get bratty about the church if it doesn't work out right away. You are looking for something special and rare: a confidant and friend.

You may also visit a pastor or a counselor, but make sure to ask for prayer.

Be transparent. Over the years, I've belonged to three small groups in which we could really be ourselves. It was always nerve-wracking, but the rewards were worth it. Sorry, but you can't get away from the nerve-wracking part: you have to risk rejection in order to gain acceptance.

Christianity is a team sport. So is prayer. If you have been defeated by Inner Mess patterns time after time, it's time to join the team.

I prayed for Jeff that day. It was just a simple prayer, asking God to deliver him from shame, to strengthen his integrity, and to quickly bring him to the woman of his dreams. And God answered. I haven't seen Jeff in a long time, but I do know he married a fantastic woman and had a lot of kids.

Maybe God is waiting for you to act like part of a body before he delivers you.

Incarnated Grace

A sobbing woman is thrown to the ground like so much garbage. Men, breathing threats of death, surround her. She covers her head and awaits her fate.

A man she has never met before speaks. 'He who is without sin among you, let him throw a stone at her first' (John 8:7).

The angry crowd evaporates, convicted by Jesus' words. The woman is too scared to notice.

Assuming she was a Jew, this woman was familiar with the Old Testament. She would understand the commandments that she and her lover had broken. She would also understand the value of a sacrifice and the work of redemption on the Day of Atonement.

But until that instruction had been hard-wired into her personality, it couldn't change her life.

Jesus left her with two statements: 'Neither do I condemn you; go and sin no more' (John 8:11).

I have no doubt that many fellow Christians would zero in on the command to sin no more and would, therefore, severely rebuke a woman like this. Or a guy like Jeff. 'He has to stop sinning, and stop right now! A good pastor would have told him so.'

Maybe.

But I can't get past the way Jesus redeemed the woman caught in adultery. His two statements are crucial, not only for their *content*, but also for their *order*.

The goal of sanctification is obedience to Christ's command, 'Go and sin no more.'

However, may I suggest that 'Go and sin no more' remains impossible until 'Neither do I condemn you' has first been instilled into our souls.

Most Christians reverse the order, with disastrous consequences. 'When you stop sinning, God will stop condemning.' The cross frees us from condemnation first, and only then will Christ enable us to go and sin no more. God always works in that order. So should Christians.

But the flesh hates this. It's stuck in the self-atonement mode, and it will fight like a bobcat before it gives up its membership card in the Flagellant Society. That is why we must incarnate God's grace. Until a flesh-and-blood human knows your faults and loves you anyway, you'll always harbor nagging doubts about God.

How tragic that so many churches – the God-given safe place for admitting the perversions of our souls – have made it so difficult to be real. I'm not advocating that we blurt out all our problems at church. But our churches should foster safe communities in which we can admit our problems to fellow pilgrims, work on them together, and pray for one another.

One caveat: do not let your Inner Mess hijack your small group or any other group. Do not impose your confession on unwilling auditors. Get permission first.

When Jeff shared his sexual struggles with me, it was the equivalent of uncovering the rotten spinach on his plate. The question that haunted him was whether or not I would still accept the plate. Would I accept him as my friend? Jeff knew the theology of God's love and grace, at least theoretically. Now he needed to know it tangibly. It was super-important, because whatever I did would reflect on God.

The people of God need to incarnate the grace of God.

I locked eyes with Jeff and told him, 'I don't have any condemnation for you over this at all.' A variation on 'Neither do I condemn you.' In that moment, I became Christ to him. I incarnated grace and Jeff not only knew it, he felt it.

We became great friends.

But it doesn't always work that way.

Dueling Inner Messes

A roomful of employees pretended not to notice the shouting match behind the closed door. The company's CEO was having it out with the president again. This time, the fight turned physical. A scuffle, then silence.

The employees had grown accustomed to these fights. Their top two company officers had a lifetime of experience of pressing each other's buttons. They were brothers.

The brothers later admitted the cause of their latest scuffle: one brother had accused the other of stealing his No. 2 pencil.

The fight ended when the combatants snapped the pencil in two.[2]

Community is a two-edged sword. It brings out our best and our worst. Ask any bickering married couple. Or bickering brothers, sisters, mothers/daughters, fathers/sons, colleagues or competitors. No one can press your Inner Mess buttons like a close friend or relative. When your Inner Mess joins the fray, it doesn't take much for the pettiest argument to become a lifelong grudge.

There are few human encounters as ugly as dueling Inner Messes. Yet God requires that we live in community. How can we create a truce when bus-to-bus warfare breaks out? Scripture offers a few solutions:

> *A soft answer turns away wrath, But a harsh word stirs up anger.*
>
> (Proverbs 15:1)

Professional hockey metes out the severest penalties, not to the players who start a fight, but to the players who join it later and keep it going. Just because your spouse or boss unleashes their flesh on you, it doesn't mean you have to respond in kind. When assailed by someone else's Inner Mess, if you are mature, you will respond in the opposite spirit. Instead of a harsh word, you offer a soft answer.

When Don, my boss at the photo-finishing store, unleashed his Inner Thug against me, God brought Proverbs 15:1 to my mind. When he had finished screaming, I answered quietly, 'Don, you're right. I'm sorry. It will never happen again.' A soft answer. The air went out of him like a punctured beach ball. Later, he called me into his office and humbly apologized. He never yelled at me again.

I wanted an apology as public as his attack, but I didn't say so:

> *Do not answer a fool according to his folly, lest you also be like him.*
>
> (Proverbs 26:4)

In England in 1792, Lady Almeria Braddock received a visit from socialite and friend Mrs. Elphinstone. When the conversation turned to Lady Braddock's age, Mrs. Elphinstone expressed skepticism at the lady's claim. Lady Braddock took offense and challenged her visitor to a duel with pistols.

Might we call this answering a fool according to her folly?

These dueling Inner Messes have gone down in history as 'The Petticoat Duel'. The ladies met at the arranged time for their Hyde Park encounter, identified their customary 'seconds', and proceeded to duel.

Upon the agreed signal, the ladies fired a single pistol shot at each other. Lady Braddock's shot missed altogether. Mrs. Elphinstone succeeded in shooting the hat from Lady Braddock's dishonored head. Despite protests from their seconds to consider the matter resolved, the ladies continued the duel.

Let the person who has never pushed an argument to idiotic extremes cast the first stone.

Or, in this case, parry the first thrust. Lady Braddock and Mrs. Elphinstone resorted to swords to settle their grudge. After a few swashbuckling moments, Lady Braddock inflicted a minor wound on Mrs. Elphinstone's arm. Mrs. Elphinstone capitulated, promising a letter of apology to Lady Braddock. The ladies exchanged pleasantries and returned home, honor satisfied.[3]

Or, should we say, Inner Messes satisfied. Your Inner Mess has mastered the art of needlessly upping the stakes. Rather than restoring a relationship or resolving a dispute, your Inner Mess savors the opportunity to escalate trivial offenses to international incidents.

Yet Scripture advises against answering a fool according to her folly. *Somebody* has to act like a grown-up and defuse the standoff. One of the duelists has to deactivate his or her Inner Mess before the bloodletting begins. Let it be you. Listen to that still, small voice of the Spirit. Dramatically change the tenor of the argument. Let God take care of your honor:

*Answer a fool according to his folly, lest he be wise in his
own eyes.*

(Proverbs 26:5)

At first glance it might seem as if the Preacher of Proverbs
just contradicted the previous verse. But not really. Verse
4 teaches how to protect yourself. Verse 5 teaches how to
confront the fool.

Case in point: King Solomon and the contested baby.
Two women claimed a baby as their own. With no means of
identifying the true mother, Solomon ordered his servants to
divide the living child in two (1 Kings 3:25). He answered a
fool according to her folly – he would not have killed the child.
His ploy worked. The real mother immediately relinquished
her claim in order to spare her child.

But what about the other woman? She illustrated the flesh
in its unvarnished malevolence. 'Let [the child] be neither
mine nor yours, but divide him' (verse 26). By answering the
fool according to her folly, Solomon forced her to manifest the
depths of her depravity. He forced the truth out of hiding and
saved the child. There is no limit to the evil that is possible
when Inner Messes duel. But there is hope.

That fraternal fight between company executives ended
when the No. 2 pencil snapped in half and the brothers began
laughing. If even one duelist can admit the ridiculousness of
most conflicts, there is hope.

Why don't you be the one?

Let it Go

Historians speak of a legendary Athenian warrior named
Cynaegiros. After the Battle of Marathon, as the Persians
departed in their boats, Cynaegiros seized an enemy vessel
with his left hand. A sailor on board lopped off Cynaegiros'
left hand with his sword. So he grabbed on with his right hand.
The sailor lopped off his right hand. So Cynaegiros grabbed
the boat with his teeth.

His headless body lay in a pool of blood on the beach as the boat sailed away.[4]

Somebody should have taught Cynaegiros when to let go.

Jesus taught, 'Agree with your adversary quickly, while you are on the way with him, lest your adversary deliver you to the judge, the judge hand you over to the officer, and you be thrown into prison' (Matthew 5:25). In other words, whenever Inner Mess duels spiral out of control, the only result is more bondage. End the madness fast.

Somebody has to tap into the power of Jesus Christ and let the offense go. Otherwise you'll keep escalating the battle until you've dissolved the marriage, wounded the child, split the church, lost the job, or wrecked the friendship.

Acknowledge your fault, however mino1r. Navigate the shoals of your adversary's Inner Mess as well as you can. Make peace wherever possible. Forbear. Forgive. Let it go.

Paul rebuked the Corinthian Christians for their duels: 'For where there are envy, strife, and divisions among you, are you not carnal and behaving like mere men [not empowered by Jesus]?' (1 Corinthians 3:3). The flesh isn't just about sex, drugs, and rock and roll. It's mainly about relationships.

The surest sign of dueling Inner Messes is broken community: envy, strife, and divisions among you. The flesh grows best in the moist, dark environment of isolation, self-pity, vengeance, passive-aggressiveness and superficiality. Your C.I.A. Agent finds isolation to be the best environment for its clandestine operations. *Confess my faults? Reveal my deep Inner Mess patterns? Reveal the voices in my head? Humble myself? Agree with my adversary? Ask for prayer? Maintain that relationship? Never!*

Your church is your team. When a team celebrates a championship victory, what do you see? You see love. You see players jumping on each other, hugging, laughing, embracing, and displaying affection they would never show in other contexts. Among top-tier teams, the difference in skill levels is microscopic. It is the difference in team unity that puts a team over the top. Love makes the difference.

Quit letting your Inner Mess poison the locker room.

One puzzle: how to solve the problem of your Inner Mess.

Five pieces: grace, the cross, the galvanizing power of Christ through the Spirit, faith, and community.

Let's put them together.

Taking Out the Trash

When was the last time you asked for prayer over an Inner Mess foul-up in your life?

How healthy is your involvement in a spiritual community? Don't answer in terms of your friendships or buddies, but in terms of your spiritually-minded friends who help buttress your faithfulness to God. Do you participate in a church?

An evangelist of the last century preached, 'There are five gospels: Matthew, Mark, Luke, John, and the Christian, and some people will never read the first four.'[5] Is there anybody in your life for whom you incarnate God's grace? If not, are you ready to change that?

Describe a time when you have escalated a trivial argument to ridiculous proportions. Which characters on your bus took the lead? What might you do differently today?

How well do your relationships display the life of Christ as described in James 3:17: 'But the wisdom that is from above is first pure, then peaceable, gentle, willing to yield, full of mercy and good fruits, without partiality and without hypocrisy.'? Rate yourself one quality at a time.

Prayer: For the courage and tenacity to connect with a church that fosters both biblical Christianity and true community.

Chapter 14
The Grace Drill

*The devil, of course, is the accuser of the brethren.
He will accuse us and make us feel condemned and
unworthy. But Paul is saying to us, 'Don't listen to the
voice of the accuser. It is God who justifies you – so no
one has any right to accuse you. Jesus Christ has already
borne our guilt. So confess your sin to God, accept His
forgiveness, and move on.*

Ray C. Stedman, 1975[1]

'Bunch of cowards. Losers.' Before anyone could react,
the felon jumped off the bus and disappeared. The hooker
dropped the gun and slumped into her seat, sobbing. The
tract lady moved beside her and put an arm around her, Scott
noticed, but without tracts.

He exhaled. Scott felt as if he'd held his breath for hours.
In reality, only minutes had passed since the felon had pulled
his stunt. He couldn't wait to get home and to hold his wife
and hug his son.

Scott turned to the heavyset woman. 'You saved our lives
today.'

'It wasn't me,' she said. 'You did it.'

Jason and Katie knelt beside the fallen cop. He stirred; the
wound seemed superficial. Jason glanced at Katie. His eyes
welled up with tears as he whispered, 'I am so sorry. We have
to talk.' With tears streaming down her face, she nodded.

The punk still hadn't moved. The old man tended him.

The heavyset woman joined in. The tract lady mouthed her prayers as she held the hooker close.

Scott hurried to call his dispatcher. He needed ambulances fast. The sound of blaring car horns irritated him. *If only they knew...* In the corner of his eye, Scott caught a movement outside his bus. It seemed as if a cab had darted into the oncoming lane to get around his bus. He shrugged it off.

A momentary quiet settled across the bus. The passengers sat barely moving, some with stunned looks, some on cell phones, some wiping away an errant tear, still others in a state of shock.

The quiet was shattered with a jolt as the unthinkable happened.

* * *

Joseph turned from the mirror in disgust. *I hate myself. How did I turn out this way?* His hair was matted with filth. His unwashed body bore the marks − and the stench − of a life spiraling out of control. Empty liquor bottles littered the room. Joseph's bleary eyes went to yet another nameless girl sprawled across his bed. He shook his head in disgust. *I hate this life. My job is miserable. I'm broke. Nobody cares. I wish I could die.*

My dad was right. I should have stayed home. I wonder if it's too late. Maybe he'll let me clean the bathrooms for one of his companies. I have to chance it. I just hope he doesn't hate me.

Little did he know that his father anxiously watched for his return every single day.

In the parable of the prodigal son, Jesus provides, once for all, the paradigm for how the Father deals with the outcroppings of our Inner Mess. If you don't know the story, take a minute and read Luke 15:11−32 in your Bible (or in the Appendix).

The word 'prodigal' refers to a lifestyle that is reckless, out of bounds, extravagant, and self-destructive. The tabloids have no shortage of prodigal celebrities. The church has its fair share of prodigal Christians, too. Every time we cave in to the Inner Mess, we become, at least for a moment, prodigal sons and daughters.

When the prodigal son came to his senses, he ran a quick cost-benefit analysis, comparing himself with his father's hirelings:

ME: flat broke, sick of partying, full of self-loathing, working at a wretched job, wracked by a guilty conscience.

DAD'S HIRELINGS: the opposite of me.

CONCLUSION: Go home.

So he returned to his father, worrying with every step whether or not his father would take him back.

In the ancient world it was said that a nobleman wouldn't run in public. Yet, as Jesus tells the story, when the father saw his son a long way off, he ran to him, embraced him, and showered him with kisses.

The story is so clear. Yet why do so many Christians resist believing that their heavenly Father will receive them with enthusiastic love when they return from a journey to the dark side? Why must we pile terms and conditions onto God's offer of forgiveness?

'And the son said to him, "Father, I have sinned against heaven and in your sight, and am no longer worthy to be called your son" ' (Luke 15:21).

Confession made. Confession accepted. Party time. *Bring out the best robe! Put the ring of authority back on his finger! Get this man some sandals. Bring out the fattened calf and let's have steaks. Give him the filet mignon! I call dibs on a ribeye.*

But, you ask, 'What about the years of prodigal living? What about blowing through his father's money? What about Responsibility and Restitution? What about the good people who never let their Inner Mess run wild? When is *their* party? The father is subsidizing bad behavior! That kid needs a good talking to.'

You have landed comfortably in the stiff working boots of the older brother, the Prince of Propriety.

He stood outside the party whining that he'd been a good

boy – a paragon of virtue – yet his father had never thrown him a party. In his view, the younger brother deserved a stern lecture followed by a lifelong wage garnishment to repay the debts he had incurred in God-only-knows-what awful kinds of debauchery.

Now whose Inner Mess is activated?

The older brother labored under the fatal misconception that life with the Father is more about doing your duty than about enjoying your relationship. The older brother's legalism was every bit as carnal as his brother's prodigality.

Both sons scorned their father's love. The only difference was that the prodigal son came to his senses and confessed it. That act immediately realigned him with his father's love in a way that left his self-absorbed brother standing outside in the T-bone-less cold.

After those messy episodes in which you've succumbed to your Inner Mess, you need to follow the prodigal son's footsteps back to your heavenly Father's love. The Grace Drill shows you how, in four steps.

Grace Drill

If we confess our sins, He is faithful and just to forgive us our sins and to cleanse us from all unrighteousness.

(1 John 1:9)

Here are four steps to resolve your flesh-induced guilt, sin, and shame.

Step One: Confess it

Confess your sin to God. When you confess your sins, God promises to forgive them.

Be careful, though. Your Inner Mess scurries feverishly to degrade the act of confession into either protracted episodes of morbid introspection or mechanical routines of religious ritual.

God doesn't want you to spend long hours hunting sins to confess. Some Christians even begin to feel guilty for *not* feeling guilty. Confession requires only that you bring to God the sins that the Holy Spirit brings to mind. The Grace Drill is supposed to clear your conscience, not burden it with long stretches of chest-pounding, self-doubting navel-gazing.

You might as well bring out the whips.

It's fine to ask God to 'search you and try your heart' but don't drag it out. Morbid introspection is as much a product of your Inner Mess as any sin you're hoping to unearth.

So is your mindless use of a confessional. Whether or not you confess your sins to a priest, you must still confess them to God. The good news is you can. You have all the authority you need to go straight to God, *sans* confessor, with your guilt. That's because every Christian is a priest (1 Peter 2:9; 1 Timothy 2:5). You need no absolution beside the forgiveness Jesus has already purchased. And you need no penance beside the penalty that he paid when he died (Hebrews 1:3).

Confession itself does not merit forgiveness; it simply realigns you with the forgiveness you already have in Christ. Whether or not you use a confessor, remember that your forgiveness rests on Jesus, not on your contrition, confession, penance or absolution.

It is at this point that your Inner Mess shifts into overdrive. The inner dialogue goes like this:

INNER MESS: That can't be all there is to it. You have to do your part too, or God won't forgive you.
NOBLE SELF: No way. Christ paid in full. There's nothing to add.
BUS DRIVER: You guys are confusing me.
INNER MESS: Don't listen to him – he's an optimist. How could any self-respecting deity let you off the hook so easily? Yeah, yeah, Jesus died and all that. But what about remorse? And restitution? And changing your life? And never doing it again? And maybe doing a mission project to help pay it off?

We need some serious *repentance* here!

BUS DRIVER: I don't know... What you say makes sense, but then there's Jesus. I thought he said, 'It is finished!'

INNER MESS: Yes, *theoretically* finished, but not really. He just got the ball rolling. Now it's your turn. At least have the decency to berate yourself for a few days. Let me gnaw at your conscience for a while. Let's at least *try* to weep, for heaven's sake. I'll settle for an honest attempt. But you'll still be guilty; remember that.

If you want to spend your days wallowing in guilt or arguing with God's final disposition of your sins, go ahead. Just don't make me listen to it. The court has decreed that the very sin that is weighing you down has been paid in full by the blood of Christ. You'd be smart to agree.

You might wonder, 'Don't I have to feel sorry for my sins? Or, shouldn't I at least promise not to do them again? Shouldn't I implore God's forgiveness?'

There is no price tag on God's forgiveness other than Jesus. Not even your sorrow, your remorse, your resolutions, your self-punishment, guilt, or shame. It's not you, it's Christ. It's all about Jesus.

There is a place for sorrow, remorse, and amending your ways. But don't let the absence of those things keep you from leaving the pig slop of a prodigal life and coming home to your Father.

That leads to the second step in the Grace Drill:

Step Two: Crossify it

This is the second step in restoring your relationship with God. God is faithful *and just* to forgive your sins. Why is he just? Because Jesus paid in full, so that for God not to forgive you would be unjust. It would be double jeopardy.

To 'crossify' your sins means to bring yourself mentally to Christ's cross and to picture the sin you have just confessed being paid in full there. Your guilt trips should last only as long as it takes for you to say, 'Thank you, Father, for the cross.'

So far, your application of the Grace Drill might sound like this:

Confess it: 'Father, I have sinned. I spoke sharply to my wife. I didn't control my temper. No excuses, God. I sinned against her and against you.'

Crossify it: 'Father, I know that Jesus paid with his life for these sins. Thank you, Father, for the cross.'

The Bible says, 'And those who are Christ's have crucified the flesh with its passions and desires' (Galatians 5:24). Earlier in the same book, Paul wrote, 'I have been crucified with Christ' (Galatians 2:20). Notice that he's not saying that you should run out and crucify yourself, as some overzealous, but misguided, Christians do. Nor does he suggest that you must go out and crucify the flesh. He's not telling you to *do* anything. He's telling you what has already been *done* for you. The crucifixion he describes is a past-tense reality for every child of God.

Your crucifixion is simply your permanent association and identification with Christ's crucifixion. His cross counts for you and you are one with him.

Since the old you has been crucified – through union with Christ – you should keep on believing it. When a sin or habit hounds you with guilt and shame, drag it right back to the cross, point at your Savior, and tell it to be quiet. It is not God's plan that you be haunted by past sins.

Crossify them.

Step Three: Contain it

Not long ago, my dog ran through poison oak. I, who am highly allergic to the stuff, didn't know. When my dog returned, I petted him and scratched his belly. Then I scratched my arm. And my leg. And my other arm, my chest, an ankle, and apparently most of my face.

Within two days, I was covered with pus-filled blisters. One eye had swollen completely shut; the other eye was on its way.

I suffered a failure of containment. I picked up a little poison oak on my hands and then spread it over most of my body.

A chain-smoker can burn through a whole pack of cigarettes on one match. One cigarette lights the next.

We are, by nature, chain-sinners. That's why we need to contain our sins. The Bible says, 'He who covers his sins will not prosper, but whoever confesses *and forsakes them* will have mercy' (Proverbs 28:13).

But you worry, 'I have some sins that I can't contain. I'm addicted to them.' I completely understand. The Bible cautions against 'easily besetting' sins (Hebrews 12:1). Certain temptations just roll off the backs of your friends, but latch onto you like a blood-starved tick.

What are your 'easily besetting' or stubborn sins? Self-righteousness, phoniness, extramarital sex, pornography, violence, drug abuse, alcoholism, lying, stealing, greed, negativity, gossip, hypocrisy, sexual sin, disrespect for authority, self-pity, arrogance, self-absorption – the possibilities are endless. Some sins on this list scarcely entice you at all; others practically own you. We're all different. We all have different 'easily besetting sins'.

How can you 'contain' them? Here are six tips – not for the containment that slaps a lid over your sins and pretends they don't exist – but the containment that foils one sin's attempt to ignite another.

1. Take total responsibility. No more blaming the devil, parents, spouse, friends, kids, victims, pastor, church, upbringing, boyfriend, girlfriend, hormones, peer group, teachers, government, bad luck, karma, the cosmos, bad genes, boss, your ex, 'the Man', enemies, or God. Think of the carnival that breaks out on your bus every time a derelict passenger scores a sin and you blame someone else. Your Inner Mess dances in the aisles even as it forges the next link in your chain of sin.

2. Run away. Some temptations aren't worth fighting. For example, the Bible says to flee sexual immorality (1 Corinthians 6:18). Don't negotiate. Don't ruminate. Don't walk. Run! Flee as soon as you spot a temptation from your 'easily besetting sin' list. A friend of mine changed jobs to get away from a woman who was trying to seduce him. You might have to install pornography filters on your Internet service. Or cut up your credit cards. Take drastic action to elude your tempter.

3. Receive prayer. Develop relationships with other Christians and don't be too bashful to ask for prayer. 'Gina, will you pray for me? I'm really struggling to keep my spending under control.' Some church leaders offer anointing with oil and prayer for particularly stubborn sins or addictions (James 5:14, 15). Find out what your church offers.

4. Join a biblically based recovery group. Crack the shell of secrecy. Expose your needy characters to the supernatural power of God. Take that courageous step and attend your first meeting of a Christian recovery or twelve-step group. Check with your church or visit the Inner Mess website for some resources.

5. Have a life beyond your struggle. Like any self-respecting toddler, your Inner Mess loves being the center of attention. So change the focus. Resist the urge to turn every conversation into therapy or a complaint session. Focus on your life's purpose, your mission, your spiritual growth, and on meeting the needs of others.

6. Stock up on Scripture. The Bible transmits more than information; it transmits God's power (Hebrews 4:12). Specifically, God's *cleansing* power (Ephesians 5:26; Psalm 119:11). Scripture is the Holy Spirit's weapon of choice to battle the evil within (Ephesians 6:17). Whenever you read, learn, study, discuss, meditate upon, sing, or memorize the Bible, you change the atmosphere on your bus. Your Inner Mess gags on Scripture like a sweet-toothed boy on vegetables. Many Bibles have a concordance – an index to keywords – at the back. Find some verses about your Inner Mess's pet sins, and load them onto your bus. Visit the Inner Mess website for lists of verses that address a variety of 'easily besetting sins'. God gave you his word, in part, to contain your sin.

Your Inner Mess is not your master – don't fall for its lie. One day soon, you will look back in amazement at how far God has brought you.

One step remains.

Step Four: Cancel it

If you have an appointment with guilt, cancel it. If you have an appointment with self-loathing or shame, cancel that too. If you have an appointment with vengeance, cancel it.

This fourth step may be the hardest for you. But it is also the most liberating. When you cancel your guilt and shame, you accept the consequences, forget the past, and move on.

Accept the Consequences. When Christians sin, there are no *judicial* consequences for us, but there are *familial* consequences. God loves us so much that he brings on the discipline (Hebrews 12:6, 7). God's discipline hurts. The prodigal son felt the pain of a life separated from his father. And so will you. But, like the prodigal son, as soon as you come back to God through the Grace Drill, God cancels the discipline. Does the suffering end? Not always.

There may be scars – long-term consequences of your sin. You have to accept them without whining, bitterness, or self-pity. You may lose money, relationships, freedom, friendships, status, privileges, health, the right to minister, your job. You may have to serve time in prison. Serve it for the glory of God.

One of my good friends spent time in a federal prison. He used that time to lead Bible studies and to direct dozens of fellow inmates to Jesus and his grace. By accepting his consequences, he converted his discipline into a source of blessing. His prison time was still a painful ordeal, but its purpose transcended his suffering. You just have to trust that God has hidden a blessing within his discipline.

As soon as you use the Grace Drill, God converts your consequences to blessings in disguise. So, accept the consequences and then…

Forget the past. Perhaps the most depressing price we pay when our Inner Mess trashes our outer world is the loss of time. Wasted years. A rich relative may restore your money. A doctor may restore your health. Counselors may restore your peace and your relationships. But who can restore lost time?

An ancient prophet records a remarkable promise from God. After God's people turned against him, God disciplined them by sending his army against them: swarms of locusts. The locusts devastated the land and the economy.

Then God sent the prophet Joel to call his people back to grace. A remarkable promise comes at the end of that call: 'So I will restore to you the years that the swarming locust has eaten…' (Joel 2:25).

The Lord of Time can make up lost time, so forget the past (Philippians 3:13, 14). Forget your past failures. Forget your past sins. Forget your past Inner Mess patterns. If you have confessed them, crossified them, and contained them, then God has forgotten them. You should too.

Of course, you can't erase your memories. But you don't have to dwell on them. What if *Paul*, the apostle, had spent the rest of his life wallowing in guilt and shame for persecuting Christians? What if *Peter* had never cancelled his shame over denying Jesus? What if *Rahab* had let years of prostitution define her? Or *the woman taken in adultery* never accepted Jesus' forgiveness?

Time after time, the Bible presents us with fallen, guilty, shameful men and women who obtain forgiveness through the grace of God. So, accept the consequences, forget the past, and then…

Move On. Don't let your past sins haunt you. As often as your Inner Mess trashes your outer world, use the Grace Drill, and move on. Seventy-times-seven times, if you need to.

Don't let your Inner Mess peck your conscience into a

woe-is-me, self-loathing, hunkered-down, auto-flagellating frenzy. Confess your sin, crossify it, contain it, and cancel it.

Do you know what makes the angels stand up and cheer? You do, every time you, like the prodigal son, come home to God (Luke 16:10). Practice the Grace Drill. Get on with your life. When your Inner Mess rears its fuzzy head, poke it in its beady, little eye.

Sooner or later, you need to discover the whole secret of the Grace Drill: because of Jesus, there is more grace in God's heart than there is sin in your heart. Discover that, and you'll almost hear the applause of heaven.

Taking Out the Trash

In the story of the prodigal son, are you more like the prodigal or the older brother?

When your conscience convicts you of sin, what has been your standard operating procedure? How well does it work for you? How does it compare with the Grace Drill?

Memorize the steps in the Grace Drill and drill them over and over: Confess it. Crossify it. Contain it. Cancel it.

List three or four 'easily besetting' sins for you. What changes can you make to your daily routine to weaken their grip on you?

What do these verses imply for the guilt that haunts you? 'No, dear brothers and sisters, I am still not all I should be, but I am focusing all my energies on this one thing: Forgetting the past and looking forward to what lies ahead, I strain to reach the end of the race and receive the prize for which God, through Christ Jesus, is calling us up to heaven' (Philippians 3:13, 14, NLT).

Prayer: For increasing confidence in the full sufficiency of Jesus' death and resurrection.

Chapter 15
Two Scripts

*If we are to bring forth fruit in the Christian life, or
rather, if Christ is to bring forth this fruit through us by
the agency of the Holy Spirit, there must be a constant
act of faith, of thinking: Upon the basis of your promises
I am looking for you to fulfill them, O my Jesus Christ;
bring forth your fruit through me into this poor world.*

Francis Schaeffer, 1975[1]

The sound of squealing tires stopped Scott dead in his tracks.
A split second later, an explosion rocked the bus sideways,
sending him and the passengers flying. Scott cracked his head
on the way down; he felt the intense heat of a fireball. Bodies
lay tangled with Scott's on the floor. Acrid smoke filled the
bus. Scott's lungs felt the caustic effects of burning plastic, as
the front of the bus erupted in flames.

Scott fought for air and clambered from beneath the
tangle of bodies. Raw fear gripped him. *Oh God! I'm not ready!
My family! Please! God!* It seemed so impossible. Hadn't they
just finished one nightmare, and now this? Could this really
be happening?

Panic-stricken passengers scrambled toward the back exit.
Most got off safely. A few good Samaritans had even dragged
the cop and the unconscious punk down the steps and off the
bus. Only a handful of passengers remained.

The smoke burned Scott's throat. The heat grew intense.
Scott shouted for everybody to get off. He coughed and tears

ran freely as the smoke grew thicker. The bus emptied fast. Scott saw Jason and the tract lady shoving others toward the exit. Even the mean drunk was tugging the old bag lady out of her seat.

Scott began nursing hope that no one would be hurt. He scanned the bus one last time. The fire was spreading from the front to the rear. Only Scott, Jason, and the mean drunk remained.

What he saw next paralyzed him with fear.

The heavyset woman lay trapped behind the twisted metal of the rear seats. The air filled with smoke. The heat was intense. Scott and the others needed to get out now. She reached out a weakened hand to them.

Silently, she waved them off the bus.

* * *

The Perfect Storm

The disciples panicked when the storm blew in. As seasoned fishermen, they were accustomed to storms. But this one was bigger than any they had seen before. This was a perfect storm. Jesus administered a mid-term exam for his disciples. Would they pass the test or would they yield to their Inner Wimps?

While the storm raged, Jesus slept (Mark 4:38).[2] He napped while his disciples freaked out and feared death. How could he be so detached?

Because Jesus knew that God had provided absolutely every resource the disciples would need for this moment. Grace. The cross. Faith. The Holy Spirit. The personal presence of Jesus. Community. Every resource was there.

But if the disciples would not avail themselves of those resources, whose fault was that? Why should Jesus disturb his own tranquility to do remedial work for people who didn't prepare when they had the chance? Jesus loved his disciples.

He would die to rescue them from their sins, but he would not disturb a perfectly good nap to rescue them from their willful spiritual immaturity.

For the disciples – as for us – the storm itself is never the root problem. Without exception, whether your Inner Mess or your outer circumstance kicks up a storm, the root problem is revealed in one question: *How is it that your faith is so small?* It is not the greatness of the storm but the smallness of the faith that energizes your problem. And whenever that is the case, true love does not get in the way. True love retires to the back of the boat and lets the storm blow full force.

The disciples rushed to Jesus: *Teacher, do you not care that we are perishing?* (verse 38). Notice the pronouns *you* and *we*. When your Inner Mess is activated, you see yourself as the sun, and everyone else as a planet, orbiting your gigantic bundle of needs.

Their question is really an accusation. Jesus' closest followers accuse him of not caring. How endearing! A Christian out of sync with God is obnoxious to behold.

The biggest wonder here is not the calming of the storm, but that Jesus could take a nap during it. In case you're tempted to dismiss Jesus' example here, remember that he restricted his use of divine powers. Jesus, the human, had built up the power to stay on offense instead of being pushed back on defense. Jesus didn't have to worry about storms; the storms had to worry about Jesus. Later he would command, 'Peace be still,' and there would be a great calm (verse 39).

The wonderfully deflating theology of this passage is that – through their own spiritual maturity, if they'd had it – the disciples could have enjoyed a nice nap too. Their problem was not the storm; it was their wimpy spiritual lives that made them kowtow to their Inner Mess. Now Jesus tells them so:

> But He said to them, *'Why are you so fearful? How is it that you have no faith?'*

> (Mark 4:40)

If we were writing the story, most Christians would have Jesus soothing the frightened disciples. Patting their little hands. 'There, there. That was a very scary storm, little bunny.' But that's only because we don't grasp the high expectations God has for us.

Jesus asks, 'Why are you so fearful?' The Greek word for 'fearful' is *deilos*, not *phobos*, the normal word for fear. *Deilos* denotes someone who is timid, intimidated, or pathetic. It means the opposite of manly.[3] In effect, Jesus asked these seasoned fishermen why they were such *sissies*.

He's a tough coach, isn't he?

Seasoned sailors, manly men, whining like sissies! The disciples had every opportunity to grow up and to be prepared for this great test. They could have passed with flying colors. They could have laughed at the storm and found peace. And the fact that they could have done all this, but didn't, makes them pathetic. Jesus was a spiritual champion. They were spiritual sissies.

And so are we, I say with lots and lots of love, whenever we succumb to our Inner Mess. But it gets worse. Jesus hasn't finished chewing out his disciples.

He asks, *How is it that you have no faith?* Explain it, if you can. God always provides for you. His grace always provides a way out, no matter how tough the trial (1 Corinthians 10:13). When the need is there, the *grace* is there. Unfortunately, the *faith* is not always there to lay hold of that grace. Why not?

The story ends with the most penetrating question of all:

> *And they feared exceedingly and said one to another,*
> *'What manner of man is this, that even the wind and the*
> *sea obey him?'*
>
> (Mark 4:41, KJ21)[4]

What manner of man is this? The story leaves the question dangling. It's a teaser. What manner of man is this? It is exactly the same manner of man and woman that every disciple of Jesus can become.

Our problem is that most days we don't believe it.

The Grace Script

Wayne worked as a cabinetmaker before he became a pastor. We had become great friends and he helped me build the cabinets in my kitchen as a wedding gift to Margi and me. Wayne told of his former boss's explosive temper. Every time Wayne made a mistake, his boss shouted, 'Stupid idiot!' Wayne heard it so often that, even years later, whenever he made a mistake, Wayne's inner voices shouted, 'Stupid idiot!'

For fun, as we built the cabinets, we shouted 'Stupid idiot' at each other's mistakes.

'Stupid idiot' became an 'inner script' for Wayne. Scripts like these crack the whip over your attitudes and behaviors. After the Grace Drill, the next step in freedom from Inner Mess domination is writing new scripts. We need to write two of them.

The first one, called the Grace Script, replaces all the 'Stupid idiot!' type voices in your head. Use this script as often as you catch your Inner Mess in the act. The Grace Drill (chapter 14) is what you say to God. The Grace Script (this chapter) is what you say to yourself. If you use it often enough, the Grace Script will become a habit. It will displace old, self-defeating scripts such as 'Stupid idiot'. It has three simple lines.[5]

Line One: Aha!
This is a word of discovery and realization. This is what you say when you catch yourself being unkind, devious, crabby, or deceitful. You say *Aha!* I see you, Inner Mess.

When the disciples panicked at the storm, they should have caught themselves. They should have said, 'Aha! We are operating in the flesh!' But they missed it. They had a second opportunity when their Inner Finger-Wagger judged Jesus for not caring. They should have said, 'Aha! Look at us, being obnoxious and carnal.'

You see your Inner mess as you see the wind: indirectly. You see it in the faces and reactions of the people who love you. So we need an *Aha!* moment. That's the first word of the Grace Script.

Line Two: Of course!

Of course implies that you're not surprised. It connotes gentleness and grace. This is crucial, because the harsher you are, the more your Inner Mess pushes back.

So your *of course* statement might sound like, 'Of course you're blanking out – this performance review is a real threat.' Or, 'Of course you want to lash out – she lied to you.'

Of course you blew it. You have hordes of disagreeable passengers rocking your bus. Are you really surprised when you catch your Inner Mess in the act?

I can almost hear an Inner Legalist shrieking: 'See! I told you! He's soft on sin!' Relax. The whole point of the Grace Script is to extirpate sin, root and all. I'm teaching you how to hate the sin but love the sinner. If you can move through the Grace Drill to the Grace Script, you're all set up for the Holy Spirit to galvanize you against further sin.

When you catch your Inner Mess acting up, you have two options. Either you will stand in front of the bus and bawl out your band of incorrigible miscreants like a peeved camp director – which would be useless – or you can invite Jesus on board to fortify your noble characters, and either transform or evict your raunchy ones. The Grace Script extends that invitation.

Of course doesn't let you off the hook. It just stops you from acting surprised.

So you might say, 'Of course I want recognition. Of course I'm afraid of abandonment. Of course I'm mad at those past wounds. Of course I can lie, cheat, and steal. I am descended from a long, long line of sinners.'

Two lines so far: Aha! and Of course!

Line Three: Now what?

Your Inner Mess has just been caught in the act of commandeering the bus. What should you do next? Whatever you answer, your objective becomes 'let us cast off the works of darkness and let us put on the armor of light' (Romans 13:12). There is no one-size-fits-all answer, but there are some general *now what* guidelines you can follow:

> • Instead of avoiding your fears, move into them.
> • Instead of playing it safe, take a risk.
> • Instead of hiding your Inner Mess, bring it into a relationship.
> • Instead of pulling away, choose a loving action, word, or touch.
> • Instead of turning passive or retreating inward, seize life and grasp your God-given birthright.
> • Instead of swallowing your wants, speak them forth. 'I want you to keep your word. I want you call me if you'll be late. I want us to control our spending.'
> • Instead of hiding your emotions, communicate them cleanly. 'I feel angry right now. That makes me sad. You're scaring me.'
> • Instead of evading the truth, put it on the table.
> • Instead of being sarcastic or indirect, speak cleanly and directly.
> • Instead of holding a grudge, forgive and forbear.
> • Instead of withholding an apology, humble yourself and keep the relationship intact.

Now what becomes your signal to do the opposite of your Inner Mess instincts. You have to upset the norm. You have to stick yourself into situations you can't control – situations in which you are weak, vulnerable, frazzled – so that God can be strong. When you are strong, he isn't. When you are weak, he is strong.

Now what invites you into patterns that are opposite to your own supposed strength.

But it's messy. You'll stumble over your words. Your rehearsed speech will get interrupted. You'll forget to say the most important part. You'll feel your heart pounding through your chest. You'll feel out of control. You'll look dumb. You'll experience rejection.

But you will feel alive. You will feel anything but numb. You will shake free from the bland, safe, sheltered, hunkered-down, vanilla, mediocre, comfortable, boring, risk-free, Christ-less, churcified, shallow, needlessly complicated life your Inner Mess craves.

'Dying to self' and 'mortifying the flesh' mean dying to the self-protective, self-pitying, self-loathing, self-justifying instincts of your Inner Mess so that your best self can emerge.

When you catch your Inner Mess in the act of sabotaging your life, what script plays in your mind? You'll either play something like Wayne's 'Stupid idiot!' script, or you'll switch to the Grace Script. 'Aha! Of course! Now what?'

Make that switch and 'be renewed by the transforming of your mind.' I'm not saying it's easy. It requires grace, the cross, faith, and community. It also requires the galvanizing power of God. Here's the script for that.

The Power Script

Any serious weight lifter knows the importance of a good spotter. My friend George was a great spotter. When I felt as if I couldn't lift the weight even one more time, George quietly cheered me on. 'Push it. Finish strong.' With two fingers, he added his strength to mine so I could force a couple more reps.

My script said, 'I can't.' George's script told me, 'You can.'

Just when you feel that you can't resist your flesh even one more time, God whispers, 'You can.' *'I can do all things through Christ who strengthens me' (Philippians 4:13)*.

Use the Power Script every time you catch yourself thinking, 'I can't.' It has only two lines, so it's easy to remember.

Line One: Oops!

You say *Oops!* whenever you recognize you have made a mistake. You've given in to your Inner Mess:

> • You've unleashed your Inner Thug and screamed at your son.
> • You've yielded to your Inner Degenerate and purchased pornography.
> • You've indulged your Inner Critic and gossiped about your neighbor's daughter who's pregnant out of wedlock.
> • You've satisfied your Inner Judge with a nasty e-mail to your pastor.

Or maybe you have not yet given in to temptation. But you're growing tired of the battle. You can't muster the strength to forgive, to share, to resist temptation, or to love the person you're mad at right now. You're resisting, but the stress level keeps escalating. You feel frustrated and want to throw in the towel.

That's when you need to say *Oops!* The reason is simple: you made a mistake. The mistake is thinking you could imitate Jesus *by your own power.* As we've seen, that's impossible.

When you feel your stress level rising, you have to catch yourself and use the Power Script. Say *Oops!* and then move on to line two.

Line Two: Okay!

Okay! tells God you are ready to let Jesus live through you and love through you. *Okay!* triggers the galvanizing power of Christ:

• Okay, Jesus, I can't love this person, so you do it through me.

• Okay, Jesus, with my own power, all I can do is condemn this person. But with your power, please accept him and forgive him through me.

• Okay, Jesus, please speak your grace through me, because I'm not feeling very gracious right now.

When you say *Okay!* you invite Jesus to do through you what you've been trying to do by yourself. You invite his power and love to shine through you.

A. B. Simpson, a fiery preacher from a century ago, taught that sanctification is 'the obtainment of faith, not the attainment of works'.[6]

He taught that the key to holiness is neither the *eradication* nor the *suppression* of your flesh. Nor is it the *imitation* of Jesus, because he set the standard too high for us.

So if it isn't eradication, and it isn't suppression, and it isn't imitation, then what is it? Simpson captured it in one word: *habitation*. Jesus inhabits you and will live through you as often as you let him. But how does his habitation become real?

> *I have been crucified with Christ; it is no longer I who live, but Christ lives in me; and the life which I now live in the flesh I live by faith in the Son of God, who loved me and gave Himself for me (Galatians 2:20).*

'I live by faith in the Son of God.' That's how.

Oops! acknowledges that you tried to be holy in your own power and failed.

Okay! invites Jesus to live through you and believes that he will. 'Okay, Jesus, it's your turn. You live, love, forgive and serve through me.' Then believe that he will, and act accordingly. It's your risky, muscular, mature faith that activates the indwelling power of Christ, fills you with the Holy Spirit, and galvanizes your life with the power of God.

Whether you feel God's power or not doesn't matter.

There is no official feeling of the power of God. In fact, the weaker we feel in ourselves, the more strongly he acts on our behalf (2 Corinthians 12:10). When you act in faith, you will most likely get weary, shed tears, break a sweat, get clammy palms, and feel confused. You will not feel a sudden infusion of super powers. You will not leap tall buildings in a single bound. You will feel *human*, but in that humanity, you will bear the power of God. You will put to silence all those voices that doubt God's faithfulness. And you will unshackle your soul from your Inner Mess.

Your job is to believe that God's promises are true enough to act like it. It wasn't the disciples' fear that disappointed Jesus. It was their cowardly actions that belied a sissified faith.

How different would that story have been if the disciples had used the Power Script during the perfect storm? It might have sounded like this:

PETER (lashed by wind and rain): We're going to die! We're all going to die! Pull harder on the oars, men! Pull for your lives!

BARTHOLOMEW (straining at the oars): I want my mommy!

JOHN (shouting above the storm): Hey, wait a minute, Jesus is with us. I'm sure he can help. I'll find him. (Fights his way to the stern of the ship)

PETER: I hope he's cooking up a miracle.

JUDAS: I told you he didn't really care about us.

JOHN (returning): You won't believe this. Guess what Jesus is doing. He's sleeping! I mean out cold, snoring, taking a nap, pillow and all. You know what that means, don't you?

BARTHOLOMEW: Yes. It means we should bend over backwards and...

JOHN (interrupting): Don't be ridiculous. His nap means that we're safe. If we were in danger, he'd be helping.

PETER: I agree. Maybe. Probably not. I'm not sure. I don't know. I'm all over the place here. What do you think, Andrew?

ANDREW: Absolutely. If he's napping, we're safe. Let's stop rowing and trust him.

PHILIP: Andrew's got my vote. We should have thought of it sooner.

JOHN: I agree. All this freaking out and panic has been a big mistake. Oops! We should have known better.

PHILIP: Okay! Jesus, we're banking on you. Guys, let's put down our oars, get close to Jesus, and take a nap.

BARTHOLOMEW: But I'm scared.

JOHN: We're all scared. Let's trust him anyway.

DISCIPLES: (huddled around sleeping Jesus, weathering the storm)

BARTHOLOMEW (whispering): Should we wake him up? I think we should wake him up. Peter, wake him up.

JOHN: Shhh! Go to sleep.

JESUS (Thirty minutes later, awakens, yawns, stretches, looks around, smiles): Nice job, guys. I'm awfully proud of you. Now let's go feed 5,000. You do it this time, okay? (To the storm) Peace, be still. (To the disciples) I'm a little hungry. What have we got?

The Grace Drill. The Grace Script. The Power Script. That's what we've got. Your Inner Mess dreads these new scripts. Learn them. Use them. Be transformed by the renewing of your mind (Romans 12:2).

You need to take only one more step to cement your victory in place.

Taking Out the Trash
....

Describe the last major 'storm' in your life. If you had been on a boat with Jesus during that storm, what would he have said to you?

What are some of the most common scripts that play in your mind? Is it more likely that they come from God's Spirit or from your Inner Mess?

Memorize the Grace Script and the Power Script. Practice using them when your Inner Mess kicks up a ruckus.

How does Romans 12:2 apply to your inner scripts? 'And do not be conformed to this world, but be transformed by the renewing of your mind, that you may prove what *is* that good and acceptable and perfect will of God.'

Prayer: For a renewed mind that listens to God more than to your Inner Mess.

Chapter 16
The Secret Weapon

'Is life not full of opportunities for learning love? Every man and woman every day has a thousand of them. The world is not a playground; it is a schoolroom. Life is not a holiday, but an education. And the one eternal lesson for us all is how better we can love.'

Henry Drummond, 1874[1]

Scott looked at Jason. 'I can't ask you to do this, but I've got to help her.' Jason glanced out of the window at Katie, looked back at Scott, and nodded. The two ran to the trapped woman. They were surprised when the drunk came with them. *Nobody's all bad,* Scott's mother had taught him.

Smoke swirled around them. The woman's breathing was labored. She coughed. 'Get off before it's too late.' Blood oozed from a scrape on her head.

'And leave my favorite passenger behind? No way.' Scott grabbed the metal handrail on the crushed seat. It burned his hand.

Jason stripped off his coat, threw it over the handrail, and pulled. Scott joined him. The drunk scooted in next to the trapped woman. He tugged on her large, black purse, which was wedged beside her. Scott yelled, 'Leave it! Get off the bus!' The drunk shouted back, 'It was jamming her hips! Juss pull!'

The heavyset woman groaned, trying to wriggle free. The drunk put his feet on the back of the chair rail and pushed as Scott and Jason pulled. Smoke burned their lungs; they couldn't budge her. Tears streaked the woman's face. 'Just leave. Save yourselves. Just leave…'

'Please God. Save her. Save us all.' Scott pulled with all his might.

The men strained against the twisted metal. Time was running out. They couldn't breathe. They couldn't see. The woman slumped sideways – she'd passed out.

'I don't think we can get her,' Jason said between fits of coughing.

'One more time,' Scott begged.

The men struggled against the seat for the last time. 'God, help us!'

Suddenly a pair of hands reached in. Then another and another. Passengers had climbed back on board to help them. Katie. The tract lady. The hooker. The old man. Together, they pulled against the broken seat. It moved slightly, and then snapped in half. The woman was free. Eager hands carried her. The passengers tumbled off the bus. Scott was last.

Safe and together, the passengers looked at each other and Scott. Slowly, they moved together and embraced. Sinners and saints. Baptized by fire. United by pain and fear.

And love.

Some time later, a paramedic shook his head as Scott told the story. 'Not too many people would have done that. You guys are heroes. That was a great rescue.'

Scott smiled. We're heroes? Somehow he felt as if he'd been rescued. 'You have no idea.'

* * *

Me First

On my very first official date with my yet-to-be wife, I ran from her screaming like a schoolgirl. I left her to fend for herself against the hissing onslaught of a provoked attacker. In my defense, the attack caught both of us by surprise. My fright-and-flight reaction was completely understandable. After all, how often does a city boy like me come face to face with a marauding wild goose?

I had planned a nice date at a local fishing hole. Chicago is not known for its pristine streams or mountain-fed lakes. So we went to the The Fisherman's Dude Ranch. The Dude Ranch offered three small trout ponds, two catfish ponds, and a cute lake. That sounds pathetic to me, now that I live in a region surrounded by rushing rivers and massive lakes. At least we were guaranteed to catch fish.

So, loaded with fishing gear, we arrived at the Dude Ranch. I put my best foot forward, eager to show this beautiful woman how manly, self-assured, and noble I was. We planned to catch a few trout, pan-fry them in lemon butter, and share a memorable date.

It was memorable all right.

We walked toward our fishing spot, smiling and goofing around as first-date couples do, oblivious to the beady eyes tracking us like the quarry we'd soon become. The attack came out of nowhere. One moment I'm the coolest guy in the world, certain I'm making a great impression on my date. The next moment, a frenzy of feathers, feet, and beak assaults me. The goose charged, flapping its massive wings, hissing like a snake, and trying to peck me where no man should be pecked.

As I said, I'm a city boy. I've even dabbled in martial arts. At that time, I'd been working out, so I was muscular and fit (having kids changes a lot of things). If a mugger had attacked us, no problem.

But this was a wild goose. So I did what any red-blooded city boy would do when being attacked by a wild goose. I screamed like a sissy and ran away, leaving Margi to fend for herself. In that moment, I could only think of myself. I exemplified my Inner Mess's Prime Directive: *Me First.*

I've had better moments.

Margi claims that I strategically positioned her between the goose and myself, but that part of the story remains under dispute.

After Margi recovered from her laugh attack, I hunted in vain for any remaining scraps of manly pride, and we continued our date. Adding insult to injury, we discovered that we had wandered too close to a nesting mother goose, thus triggering a fatherly display of goose virility. *Great,* I thought. *I've been outmanned by a goose.*

I would like to think that, after a couple of children and many years of marriage, I would react differently. I'm confident I would. In my heart, I would slay a dragon to protect my wife and children. I would put myself in harm's way for them. I would give my life for them.

I would even go nose to beak with a wild goose.

Self-sacrificing love, in the final analysis, is the secret weapon that keeps your Inner Mess from trashing your outer world:

> *For you, brethren, have been called to liberty; only do not use liberty as an opportunity for the flesh, but through love serve one another.*

> (Galatians 5:13)

Your Inner Mess subscribes to a 'Me First' philosophy of life. Scripture commands us to overcome that tendency. 'Through love serve one another.' I need to point out, however, that Paul's command to love comes *after* an in-depth discussion of the power of Christ in you and walking in the Spirit.

Love is tough because our self-centeredness goes clear to the bone. It's instinctive. Any old marauding goose can trigger a mindless spasm of Me-First behavior. We're just doing what comes sub-naturally.

That's why Scripture exhorts us to *cultivate* love.

Every time you perform loving deeds of service, you baffle your Inner Mess. Your poor flesh doesn't know what to do. It malfunctions. It loses power over your life. Love does to your Inner Mess what kryptonite does to Superman.

'Aaargh,' you say, scratching your head. 'It sounds like you're putting the burden right back on me. It's what I've heard all my life: if you want to be a good Christian, you have to be – uh – a good Christian.'

No. This time it's different. This time we know that God's love stands ready to flow through us. We know about the supernatural resources that enable true love: grace, the cross, faith, the galvanized life, community.

This love is the fruit of the Spirit; it is the power of God. It's what happens when Jesus ministers to the characters on your bus.

Please don't think that this chapter's exhortation to love undermines all that I've taught about grace. God's grace must empower your love, or it isn't biblical love.

But grace doesn't absolve you of responsibility; it empowers you to fulfill your God-given responsibility.

Who's Got the Love Monkey?

Our friend Jennifer dropped a bombshell on my wife when she announced that Michael, her husband, wanted a divorce. We were 'couples' friends. We had dined together as couples many times. We were surprised they were splitting up.

We were even more surprised at the reason. Jennifer had gained weight and her husband no longer felt attracted to her. So he wanted a divorce.

It's a cold, cruel Inner Mess-trashed world out there.

An insightful business article I had read offered some perspective. 'Management Time: Who's Got the Monkey?' was published in the *Harvard Business Review* in 1974.[2] It ranks as the second most-requested article in that venerable publication's history.

Though not written about love, the article suggests a biblical way of looking at it. The authors use monkeys to represent *responsibilities*. Every organization has them. In a healthy business – or marriage – the right monkeys sit on the right backs and each monkey is properly tended. Most importantly, in a healthy organization, coworkers never shift their monkeys to someone else's back. Your monkey is your monkey – take care of it until you've discharged your responsibility.

Attraction Love

In healthy relationships, who's got the love monkey? Who owns the responsibility for nurturing and sustaining love? That answer may surprise you.

The lover, not the beloved, owns the love monkey.

Unfortunately, Michael shooed his love monkey onto Jennifer's back. Michael made her responsible for his love. As long as she remained skinny (her responsibility), Michael would love her (now also her responsibility). When her attractiveness faded – as physical attractiveness invariably does – Michael's love faded too. In Michael's mind, the monkey was on Jennifer's back.

It is perfectly valid to use attractiveness as a criterion for establishing a relationship. Most relationships, even friendships, start because of a mutual attraction. Common interests. Shared outlook. Physical beauty. Sense of humor. Many qualities attract us to others, and this is good.

Let's call this 'attraction love'.

Attraction love depends on qualities in the beloved: looks, money, brains, vivacity, sensuality, physique, humor, style, portfolio, political views, spiritual commitments.

So far, so good. Attraction love starts with the beloved. But for it to last, it can't stay with the beloved. At least not completely. As love matures, the lover owns the love monkey more and more. That, too, is good. Until the Inner Mess steps in.

The Inner Mess works hard to shoo the *lover's* monkey onto the *beloved's* back. I'll do anything to make you responsible for my love, and will justify myself – and even wrap myself in the Christian flag – in the process. You have to flawlessly say the right words, maintain your figure, earn enough money, stroke my ego, bring home the bacon, and leap through hurdles, or else I will stop loving you. And, in the enchantingly delusional thinking of my Inner Mess, on the day I stop loving you, it will be all your fault.

No two people can *always* be attracted to each other. Stressful days at the office, colicky babies and aging take their toll. Figures sag. Passions wane. Good times grow dull. The routine sets in. When you've deposited your monkey on your beloved's back, your love will evaporate as fast as you can say, 'I told you to put the seat down.'

Michael's policy with Jennifer became: *You must attract me or else I'll stop loving you. The monkey is on your back, not mine. Lose some weight and maybe you'll attract some more love out of me.* This is the inherent instability of attraction love.

Your Inner Mess only magnifies this. Its 'Me-First' instinct treats people as objects to be used and discarded when their purpose is served. While they scramble to fulfill your expectations, your Inner Mess reclines like Cleopatra in a litter, waiting for grapes of pleasure to be dropped into its maw and blaming your partner when love fails.

This explains why an ex-spouse, ex-boyfriend, or ex-girlfriend – the very one who used to light up your life and stir your loins – now makes you shake your head in wonder that you could ever love such a loser. This also explains why we can be so good at picking lousy partners over and over again: you keep delegating the choice to your Inner Mess.

The flesh loves only an *image*, never a *person*. So you craft a partner in your ideal image, convince yourself his or her sweat won't stink, and fall in love with unreality. Relationships become disposable commodities in an endless quest to satisfy an insatiable Inner Mess. Attraction love neither bears all things, nor believes all things, nor hopes all things, nor endures all things. Under the domination of your Inner Mess, you will throw today's beloved overboard in a flash if someone else wins the attraction game.

You've parked your love monkey on the wrong back.

Don't get me wrong; attraction love is a good love. It draws us together. It finds our friends for us. It's just not the ultimate love. It never can be for us flesh-afflicted humans. Thank God for a second kind of love.

Virtue Love

A spiritually healthy follower of Jesus willingly embraces the love monkey. My love for my wife and kids, by rights, depends on me, not them. The love monkey belongs on my back. Though he wouldn't accept it, Michael's love monkey for Jennifer belonged on his back.

Whether you must love a crabby spouse, a forgetful father or a piggish roommate, the principle doesn't change: the love monkey remains yours to carry, to tend, and to nourish.

Call this love *virtue love*. My love for you is not based on your current lovability, but on my virtue. Attraction love finds its source in the attractiveness of the beloved. Virtue love finds its source in the virtue of the lover.

Your capacity for virtue love, therefore, depends on your level of spiritual growth. Grow in the Lord. Grow in grace. Put away childish things (1 Corinthians 13:11). Don't wallow in a spiritual kindergarten all your days; cultivate a mature faith. Let Christ be formed in you. Radiate his love.

Virtue love fully embraces the love monkey and its responsibilities. I love you because I have developed the inner virtue and integrity to do so, no matter what you do or don't do. Even if you forget my birthday, blab my secret, or wreck my car. Even if you pack on a few pounds.

When couples recite their marriage vows – especially traditional ones – they permanently embrace the love monkey. *For richer, for poorer; in sickness and in health; to love and to cherish; till death do us part.* This is not a vow to feel mushy, but a vow to love no matter how we feel.

Attraction love is a wonderful gift, but only virtue love will stick. Which love resembles the love of Jesus?

From the depths of his heart, Jesus loved the unlovely. He looked your Inner Mess squarely in its multiple, beady eyes, and loved you anyway. He loved the total you, the real you, the unvarnished you. The whole blue-plate special. He didn't love you because you attracted him. He loved you because he joyfully accepted the love monkey and spent a lifetime nurturing his own ability to love.

Now, by grace, it's your turn.

Jesus reduced the complex laws of God to a simple, all-embracing lifestyle: love. It is the antithesis of the Inner Mess.

If Jesus commands a life of self-giving love, don't you think he stands ready to empower that love? Let Jesus love your cranky husband through you. Offer him your mouth, that he might speak kind words to your grouchy wife. Give him your hands to serve your peeved in-laws. Lend him your arms to hug a critic, your wallet to enrich an undeserving stranger, your ears to listen to a self-absorbed neighbor, and your fattened calf to celebrate a prodigal coming home.

You might even offer him your body to be pecked by a wild goose.

But I Don't Feel Like It

None of this really counts unless you do it *when you don't feel like it*. Jesus taught that the acid test of love is the love you don't feel like giving (Matthew 5:46; Luke 6:42). That's the beauty of the Power Script. Give Jesus the okay to love through you, believe that he will, and then act as if he will. And he will, even if you don't feel it. Even when your Inner Mess clamors for a fight. That's when your virtue love, borne of muscular faith, energized by Christ within, gains you the most reward.

At the risk – okay, the certainty – of pushing the monkey analogy too far, we can say that a) *love* is the monkey on your back, and b) *you* are the monkey on Jesus' back. Of course, your flesh does its nefarious utmost to knock the love monkey off your back and you off Jesus' back. Which is why you have to 'pursue love' by growing mature as a follower of Christ (1 Corinthians 14:1).

Jesus himself turns out to be your Inner Mess Terminator (of its dominance, not its presence) and virtue love is his secret weapon. The reason may surprise you.

All You've Ever Wanted

Why is a thug a thug? Why does a critic criticize? Why does your Inner Jerk pick on people? What motivates your Inner Sinner? Your Inner Dummy? Your Inner Felon?

If you were to dig through all the contradicting desires and needs within, what baseline motivation would you find? What pursuit is really driving the bus of your life?

Love.

I know it sounds sappy. But every twisted soul – and every twisted character within each twisted soul – is only seeking that ultimate connection for which God created it: authentic love with a person who knows us deeply.

When a young girl gets pregnant out of wedlock, what is she really looking for?

When a teenage boy misbehaves in class, what is he looking for?

When a lonely woman picks up strangers in a bar night after night, what is she looking for?

What about the overachieving millionaire who dropped dead at the age of fifty-one from a stress-induced heart attack?

Yes, I know, they're looking for money, pleasure, wealth, and prestige. But the more you dig, the more you realize these motivators themselves are motivated by love. Even criminals commit their crimes in a deranged pursuit of love.[3]

Underneath all your Inner Mess clutter cowers an unloved heart. So you manipulate, cajole, enforce, hint at, control, criticize, condemn, deny, excuse, whine, act out, divorce, beg, borrow, steal and try to buy that which money can't buy.

Missionary and author Oswald Chambers pointed out

that temptation suggests 'a possible shortcut to the realization of my highest goal...'[4] He was right. Though your Inner Mess longs for love, it has dismissed true love as utterly out of reach. So, instead of growing and building the virtue that leads to love, your Inner Mess looks for shortcuts. Instant gratification. If you let it, your flesh will waste an entire lifetime running up dead ends in pursuit of drive-through love.

What would happen at the back of your bus if your love life flourished? What would happen if the love of God were poured out in your heart? If you genuinely grew in love for God and your neighbor? How would your Inner Mess react?

It would quiet down. The more the love of Christ flows through you, the more you silence the love-starved voices on your bus. The more you stop your Inner Mess from trashing your outer world.

In fact, your growing experience of virtue love does even more. When it flows out of a maturing heart – out of growing experiences of grace, the cross, faith, the Spirit, and the indwelling Christ – your love life actually cleans out the accumulated garbage of a lifetime. It not only stops your Inner Mess from trashing your outer world *today*, it also purifies your heart from the debris piles of *yesterday* (1 Peter 1:22).

So right now is an excellent time to quit focusing on your Inner Mess and to start focusing on the hurting world around you. Cultivate love. Embrace the love monkey. Through love, serve one another. It's Jesus' secret weapon.

Let Jesus

A famous Bible teacher once asked his students: What is the most important word in the Bible? They shouted out their answers: grace, faith, trust, love, obey, truth, salvation, Jesus. The teacher answered that these were all great words. But they weren't the most important word.

The most important word in the Bible, he said, is the little word *let*.

Let the peace of Christ rule in your hearts (Colossians 3:15).

Let this mind be in you, which was also in Christ Jesus (Philippians 2:5).

Let your gentleness be known to all (Philippians 4:5).

Let your conduct be worthy of the gospel of Christ (Philippians 1:27).

Let Jesus board your bus. Let him meet each of your Inner Mess characters. Let him embrace them, redeem them, forgive them, purify them, and transform them. Let him integrate your transformed characters into a Christ-centered, unified identity.

Can Jesus handle all those characters at the back of your bus? Let him.

Can he love your imperfect husband, imperfect wife, imperfect children, imperfect parents, imperfect boyfriend or girlfriend, and imperfect friends through you? Let him.

Can he deliver you from a lifetime of sick scripts and destructive addictions? Let him.

Can he keep your Inner Mess from trashing your outer world? Let him.

You have all the resources you need. You have supernatural provision for every temptation. You have a life in the Spirit, an identity in Christ, and a maturing faith. You have the keys to your life's bus. You decide who drives. Put your noblest self behind the wheel. Jesus wants to empower you, hang out with you, navigate for you, and cheer you on.

He's ready to go.

Are you?

Taking Out the Trash

Have you ever been attacked by a marauding goose? Can you sympathize with me? If not, describe a time when you reacted with a blatantly 'Me First' instinct at the expense of others.

Reflect on your closest relationships and ask, 'Who's got the love monkey?' Which are you practicing more, attraction love or virtue love? How evident is your Inner Mess's 'Me First' instinct?

Are you on the path toward spiritual maturity? Are you growing in the Lord? Your love life is only as strong as your spiritual maturity (1 Corinthians 13:11). Do you need to change any spiritual habits?

What would a strong love life do to your Inner Mess? How would you change?

What is the role of love in these verses? 'Therefore, as God's chosen people, holy and dearly loved, clothe yourselves with compassion, kindness, humility, gentleness and patience. Bear with each other and forgive whatever grievances you may have against one another. Forgive as the Lord forgave you. And over all these virtues put on love, which binds them all together in perfect unity' (Colossians 3:12–14, NIV).

Prayer: That the love of Christ would flow through you, deliver you from Inner Mess dominance, and reach a hurting world around you.

Chapter 17
Inner Mess Frequently Asked Questions (FAQs)

It is so easy when you have many graces and many virtues to say, 'Christ can save me.' Yes, but when your follies stare you in the face, when your sins rebuke you, still to say 'Wash me, and I shall be whiter than snow; purge me with hyssop, and I shall be clean,' this is faith indeed.

Charles H. Spurgeon, 1862

Why don't churches teach more about the flesh?

I can't speak for other pastors, but I can for myself: it's hard for me to teach about the Inner Mess because I haven't mastered the stuff I'm teaching. I'm still in God's sanctification classroom, so my Inner Mess confronts me at every turn: 'Who are you to tell people how to stop trashing their outer world? What do you know? Look at your life!' The Inner Mess itself makes the Inner Mess a very easy topic to avoid.

Plus, the whole topic comes across as 'negative' and most of us flock toward the positive. How many Christians will sit still for teaching that tells them they're pretty messed up?

I also have a hunch that, in our race to the *practical* side of Christianity, many church leaders have left the *theological* side in the dust. Yes, there are excellent exceptions. But the trends seem to be away from the kind of systematic, in-depth teaching it takes to do justice to a topic like the Inner Mess.

The Inner Mess seems to be a complex, meddlesome,

negative, theological, guilt-inducing, self-sabotaging topic. Fortunately, once you view your Inner Mess in the mirror of Scripture, you also discover the supernatural resources to unbury your life from the debris of a lifetime.

What key Scriptures address the Inner Mess?

Look for Scripture passages that talk about the flesh, sin, the old nature, or the sinful nature, depending on your translation. Here are some key passages:

Passages with extended discussions about the flesh: Romans 5:12–21, 7:14–25, 8:1–13; Galatians 5:16–26.

Passages about the 'old man (person)' or our 'past lifetime': Romans 6:6; Ephesians 4:22; Colossians 3:9; 1 Peter 4:3.

Passages about a generally evil or willful heart: Deuteronomy 29:19; Jeremiah 7:24, 17:9; Ephesians 2:2; 2 Peter 2:10; 3:3; Jude 18.

Passages about the mental aspects of the Inner Mess: Romans 1:28, 8:7; Ephesians 4:17; Colossians 1:21, 2:18; Titus 1:15.

Other passages: Galatians 6:8; 1 John 2:16.

Why do you use the term 'Inner Mess' instead of 'flesh' or 'old sin nature'?

I coined the term 'Inner Mess' because it conjures a picture of what I'm talking about. When I use terms such as 'the flesh' or 'carnal,' most people think of drugs, sex, and rock and roll. Others, like me in my younger years, think of the physical body, presumed (incorrectly) to be evil.

However, the Scriptural concept is much deeper and more pervasive. The flesh leaves its slimy footprints on all our relationships, on our walk with God, and on a host of malfunctions within.

The terms 'old nature', 'sinful nature', and 'old sin nature' are fine, except that they sometimes say too much. I want to avoid suggesting a separate entity, like a parasite or alien, lurking within. You are a complex unity.

What's the alternative to the Inner Mess? Who else is riding on my bus?

Your human spirit, not to be confused with the Holy Spirit. I call it your Noble Self. This is you at your best, under the influence of the Holy Spirit, displaying the life and character of Christ.

The Bible calls this 'the new man'. '...[P]ut on the new man [person] which was created according to God, in true righteousness and holiness' (Ephesians 4:24). Every Christian is a new person with a new core. This core consists of you plus Christ; you fused to Jesus (Galatians 2:20). It's the best 'you,' the person you always dreamed of becoming. By faith, act like that person. Put on that new person.

God didn't obliterate your personality or turn you into a 'Stepford Christian' when you received Jesus. Instead, he added the color to your personality and brought out the very best that has always been in you. You're still you, only better.

Plus, you're never alone. Picture your inner characters, at a picnic, running a three-legged race, tied to Jesus. The more you practice, the less you stumble; the more in sync you become with Jesus.

Your new nature comes pre-wired for true righteousness and holiness. Unlike your Inner Mess, your Noble Self inclines *toward* the W.W.J.D. lifestyle. It interfaces with the Holy Spirit who indwells you. You just need to supply a consistent stream of faith to activate it. And that depends on your level of maturity (Romans 10:17; Hebrews 4:2; John 17:17).

Can you go more into the theology of the Inner Mess?

Over 230 years ago, Augustus Toplady penned a hymn, perfectly capturing the twin malfunctions that constitute the Inner Mess. In 'Rock of Ages', the hymnwriter sings to Jesus and asks him to:

> *Be of sin the double cure,*
> *Save from wrath and make me pure.*

Why a 'double cure'? Toplady knew that the flesh squats at the intersection of two sin-induced maladies: guilt and depravity. Hence the double cure: 'save from wrath [guilt] and make me pure [depravity].' For background, let's rewind to the dawn of creation.

For his own sovereign reasons, God chose to judge the human race not based on our individual performance but on the performance of our representative. Adam stood as our first representative. We were, in effect, in Adam's loins when he made his tragic choice.

Paul affirms that when Adam sinned, we all sinned (Romans 5:12–17). Don't worry about the fairness of it – it's actually God's way of treating us better than we deserve.

On the day Adam sinned, he suffered two immediate consequences. His *status* before God became guilty, and his *personal being* became corrupted. That corruption of his being affected his mind, will, emotions, body, soul, and spirit. It distorted every aspect of his life and triggered the processes of decay and death.

Both maladies cry out for a cure.

Every descendant of Adam is born with the same moral profile as fallen Adam. The combination is deadly. Meet Original Sin. No wonder Paul warned, 'For as in Adam all die…' (1Corinthians 15:22).

Your flesh, your Inner Mess, is the shrapnel that flew when your imputed guilt collided with your inherited corruption. It tore apart your soul and polluted your virtue. It all goes back to Adam, and like him, you need the Rock of Ages' double cure. The wounded, bleeding, dying, rising Jesus provided it in full.

First, by his sacrificial, substitutionary death, he saved you from the guilt of sin. He changed your status from *condemned* to *justified*. When you received him as Savior, Jesus became your new representative. You no longer fit fallen Adam's profile; you now fit the profile of Jesus Christ. That means that God will evaluate you according to Christ's righteousness, not your own.

Your deliverance from the *guilt* of sin is a past-tense, once-for-all accomplishment, and is the first part of Jesus' cure.

The second part addresses your *corruption*. By rising from the dead and coming to live inside you, Jesus immediately transforms your core identity; he puts new license plates on your bus, and climbs on board. Then he works to continually deliver you from sin's corruption. He makes you pure – over time. He brings tough love onto your bus, and repairs your malfunctioning body, soul, spirit, mind, will, and emotions. This part of the cure is an ongoing, present-tense reality. And it depends on Jesus just as much as the first part.

That's why the Bible calls him 'the Last Adam' who became, for us, 'a life-giving spirit' (1 Corinthians 15:45).

Why doesn't God just erase the Inner Mess when we receive Jesus?

Can I get back to you on that? We don't really know why, because the Bible has not told us. We do know, however, that when we meet Jesus, he will instantaneously complete that job, 'in a moment, in the twinkling of an eye' (1 Corinthians 15:52, 53).

How can you say that we should 'grace' our Inner Mess? Doesn't the Bible tell us to 'die to self'?

The alternative to gracing your Inner Mess is judging it, and I've spent enough of my life doing that to know it only makes things worse. Imagine a tribunal at the back of your bus, handing down guilty verdicts and prison sentences. Then what? How will you incarcerate your passengers? How will you execute a death sentence? What exactly are the steps involved in 'mortifying the flesh' and 'dying to self'?

But, you argue, *Scripture commands it:* 'Therefore put to death your members which are on the earth: fornication, uncleanness, passion, evil desire, and covetousness, which is idolatry' (Colossians 3:5). 'For if you live according to the flesh you will die; but if by the Spirit you put to death the deeds of the body, you will live' (Romans 8:13). *Aren't you contradicting these verses?*

Not at all. These verses command you to put to death certain *behaviors*, not your 'self' or parts of your self. Your old self – you plus zero – has already been crucified with Christ (Galatians 2:20, 5:24). There's no part of your *identity* left to crucify. There are, however, many *behaviors* that need the ax.

Grace is an *attitude of kindness* toward the sinner. You have to love the sinner *within you* though you hate the sin. But grace also becomes the *power to transform* the sinner. Dying to self means dying to any pretension that you can achieve God's holy standards by your own effort. It means giving up and casting your confidence on Christ.

That's what I mean by gracing the Inner Mess. Be hard on sin, soft on the sinner. Draw on God's power to subdue your Inner Mess passions. And have the muscular, yielded, maturing faith to keep reckoning yourself dead to sin but alive to God.

How does salvation affect my relationship with the Inner Mess?

Before salvation: you are 'in the flesh' (Romans 8:9). This means that your Inner Mess formed the nucleus of your identity.

After salvation: you are 'in Christ' (2 Corinthians 5:17). This means that your new connection with Jesus now forms the nucleus of your identity. But the flesh is still in you.

Salvation deposes your tyrannical Inner Mess, but doesn't eliminate it. It changes your identity from flesh-dominated to Christ-centered. When God saved you, he freed you from sin's authority. As he sanctifies you, God frees you from sin's power.

What's wrong with will power?

Go buy a platter of the most fattening, delicious dessert you can imagine, lock yourself in a private room, and repeat the question. If you don't have a sweet tooth, change the illustration to your area of weakness – pornography, judgmentalism, alcohol, or a pile of someone else's money.

Sheer human will power, unaided by the power of God, can never accomplish that which pleases God. 'For it is God who works in you both to will and to do for His good pleasure' (Philippians 2:13).

What will it feel like when God's power flows through me?

Whatever you're feeling like right now. When the power of God flows through you, you can feel brave or scared, strong or weak, glad or sad, happy or depressed, tender or angry. There is no official feeling of the power of God. This is what makes faith so important.

There's an apparent paradox. When Paul describes his missionary work in Colosse, he says that he labored – he put forth effort, he broke the sweat, he got tired, he did the striving – but it was by 'God's working which worked in [him] mightily' (Colossians 1:29). In other words, even though Paul felt the weight of the work, he still affirms that God did the work through him.

Your Inner Mess longs for fireworks. God delights in faith.

To the Christians in Corinth, Paul asserts that he out-labored all the other missionaries, 'yet not I, but the grace of God which was with me' (1 Corinthians 15:10). He was like an empty glove; God was the hand that filled him.

When you use the Power Script, go forth boldly to do whatever must be done, and say whatever must be said, trusting that God will work through you. Yes, you'll get tired. You'll feel depleted. You'll experience every human emotion. But at the end of the day, you will give thanks to God, who 'work[s] in you what is well pleasing in His sight, through Jesus Christ, to whom *be* glory forever and ever. Amen' (Hebrews 13:21).

For more FAQs...

Please visit our online community at www.innermess.com.

You can find more FAQs, submit your own questions, and help others with theirs.

Chapter 18
Inner Mess Glossary

*You see the struggle, but not the end; you see the campaign,
but not the reward; you see the cross, but not the crown.
You see a few humble, broken-spirited, penitent, praying
people, enduring hardships and despised by the world; but
you see not the hand of God over them, the face of God
smiling on them, the kingdom of glory prepared for them.*

J.C. Ryle, 1816–1900

Adamic nature: Often used as a synonym for the flesh, though they are not exactly identical. Your Adamic nature is your pre-salvation identity; the same as the 'old man/self' in Ephesians 4:22 and Colossians 3:9. Your flesh is one part of that identity. You inherit the exact profile of fallen Adam: a guilty status before God plus an all-pervasive corruption within your being. With this nature, you are inclined toward sin and away from a W.W.J.D. lifestyle. You also fall under God's condemnation (1 Corinthians 15:22). When you receive Jesus, you receive a new nature and a new identity.

Annihilate the Ego: An unbiblical teaching popular in the late twentieth century. This teaching identified the flesh with the ego, the self. It then applied Scriptures about crucifying the flesh, suggesting that the way to sanctification was to annihilate the ego – to die to self. I was reared with this teaching, and now have a visceral reaction against it. Most of its error stems from semantic confusion. The flesh is not the ego, and your ego – or self – is not, in itself, evil. The point of Christ's redeeming

243

work is the healing of your ego, not its annihilation. Through Christ, God exalts you – ego and all – to the throne of your life, under the influence of Christ within (Romans 5:17). God wants strong-willed men and women who freely respond to the Lordship of Jesus.

Carnal/carnality: Carnal means 'flesh-dominated.' The noun 'flesh' translates the Greek word *sarx*. The adjective 'carnal' translates the Greek word *sarkikos* or *sarkinos*. 'Flesh' and 'carnal' are the same word, except that one is a noun and the other an adjective. For example: 'For you are still carnal. For where there are envy, strife, and divisions among you, are you not carnal and behaving like mere men?' (1 Corinthians 3:3). Carnality is a state of being dominated by the flesh. In common parlance, carnality refers mainly to sexual sins. But in biblical usage, carnality refers equally to sexual sins, relationship breakdown, religious hypocrisy, and drug or alcohol addiction (Galatians 5:19–23).

Christian/Christianity: True Christianity is manifesting your new life in Christ, which you received at salvation through faith alone in Christ and his finished work on the cross. This new life consists of Jesus himself living in you. He continually generates Christ-like behavior, as you exercise faith in the inner working of the Spirit of God and the word of God, motivated by a love and desire for the glory of God.

[I've modified this definition from Ray Stedman's definition in an article called 'Legalism' at www.raystedman.org/misc/legal.]

Depravity: Mankind's state of moral failure, spiritual brokenness, and willful rebellion against God. Depravity is another term for our fallenness. Depravity reaches into every aspect of our human nature: mind, will, emotions, body, soul, and spirit. It renders us incapable of pleasing God, reaching God, or even seeking God without his initiative and personal assistance (Romans 3:10–18).

Fall, The: The terrible, horrible, no-good, very bad day when Adam sinned and plunged the world of mankind into sin and death. The Inner Mess is the result of the fall. It brought about a corruption of our nature and elicited God's curse on the entire cosmos (Romans 8:19–21).

Filling of the Holy Spirit: The antidote to carnality (Inner Mess dominance). 'I say then: Walk in the Spirit, and you shall not fulfill the lust of the flesh' (Galatians 5:16). The Holy Spirit indwells every child of God (Romans 8:9). But you can ignore him, vex him, and disobey his promptings. Resisting God's Spirit is equivalent to handing your bus keys to the Inner Mess. You immediately fall under the sway of your flesh. Even so, the Holy Spirit always stands ready to restore his influence in your life. Confess your sin through the Grace Drill, ask the Holy Spirit to fill you, and trust that he will (Luke 11:13).

Flesh, The: The Bible uses the word 'flesh' in six distinct ways. You have to look carefully at a verse's context to determine which meaning the author had in mind:

> • The substance of which the body of an animal or human is made (1 Corinthians 15:39; Genesis 2:21).
> • The whole body (Genesis 40:19).
> • A common term for all living things, both human and animal: 'All flesh is as grass' (1 Peter 1:24).
> • The material or physical aspect of a being, in contrast to the immaterial or spiritual, as in 'flesh and blood' (1 Corinthians 15:50).
> • A relative, one's own 'flesh' (Genesis 37:27).
> • The morally fallen aspect of our human nature; the Inner Mess, the subject of this book. [Adapted from the *International Standard Bible Encyclopedia*, 1939, Flesh].

As I define it, your Inner Mess (the flesh) is the garbage dump of your soul. It is the dumping ground for your morally fallen desires, drives, thoughts, beliefs, instincts and habits – all the parts of you that resist God. Left unchecked, your Inner Mess trashes your outer world, contaminates your relationships, spoils your achievements, and makes your life stink.

Grace Drill: The solution to post-salvation sin and guilt. The Grace Drill applies God's promise in 1 John 1:9: 'If we confess our sins, He is faithful and just to forgive us our sins and to cleanse us from all unrighteousness.' It outlines four action steps for your guilt and sin: Confess it, crossify it, contain it, and cancel it.

Grace Script: The mental script you use when you catch your Inner Mess in the act. Instead of berating yourself, use the Grace Script often enough that it becomes second nature. It has three lines: *Aha!* I see you, Inner Mess. *Of course!* I understand myself. I am not surprised by my own ability to sin. *Now what?* How can you alter a pattern of messed up decisions? How can you move into your fears? How can you deepen your relationships? How can you alter a pattern of messed-up decisions?

In Christ: A biblical phrase for union with Christ (described below). Also, 'in him'. For example: 'There is therefore now no condemnation to those who are in Christ Jesus, who do not walk according to the flesh, but according to the Spirit' (Romans 8:1) and 'and you are complete in Him, who is the head of all principality and power' (Colossians 2:10).

Justification: The judicial act of God in which he declares a sinner to be righteous because of the imputed righteousness of Jesus Christ. Justification is one of the blessings you received the very moment you accepted Jesus as your Savior. It is part of your spiritual portfolio of divine assets. You don't earn justification through your good deeds or your religious performance; you receive it through faith: 'When people work, their wages are not a gift. Workers earn what they receive. But people are declared righteous because of their faith, not because of their work' (Romans 4:4, 5, NLT).

Power Script: A mental script you can use when you are sufficiently frustrated by your inadequate human power. This script has two lines. After you've beaten your head against the wall a couple of times, you say, *Oops!* I've blown it by relying on my own power, apart from Christ, to love, serve, live, cope, understand, or act. Next, say, *Okay!* and invite Jesus Christ to work through you by his power. Then, trust that he will. Take whatever steps you must, and do so with confidence. The Power Script relies on Galatians 2:20: 'I have been crucified with Christ; it is no longer I who live, but Christ lives in me; and the life which I now live in the flesh I live by faith in the Son of God, who loved me and gave Himself for me.'

Sanctification: The logical follow-up to justification. Sanctification is the process by which God makes us holy. He increasingly conforms us to the character and likeness of Christ. Sanctification puts your Inner Mess out of business in three phases:

> • Phase one: at the moment of salvation, God unites you with Christ, grabs the bus keys from your Inner Mess, and hands them back to your new nature, to your Noble Self. Phase one is past-tense salvation from the penalty of sin.
> • *Phase two:* throughout the rest of your life, God continually works out Christ's holiness through your words, thoughts, actions, and character. Jesus lives in and through you – counteracting your Inner Mess, and keeping your *Noble Self* in the driver's seat. Phase two is present-tense salvation from the power of sin.
> • *Phase three:* at the moment you meet Jesus, either in death or at his return, God instantaneously completes the process of sanctification, heals your brokenness,

and eradicates every trace of sin in you. Phase three is future-tense salvation from the very presence of sin.

You'll find all three phases in verses such as Titus 2:11–13: 'For the grace of God that brings salvation has appeared to all men [phase one], teaching us that, denying ungodliness and worldly lusts, we should live soberly, righteously, and godly in the present age [phase two], looking for the blessed hope and glorious appearing of our great God and Savior Jesus Christ' [phase three].

Union with Christ: The biblical teaching that every person who receives Jesus becomes one with Christ. God joins you to Christ – he fuses you, glues you, unites you, bonds you to him – so much so that whatever is true of Jesus in his human nature before the Father also becomes true of you. You share Christ's possessions, status, identity, history, and destiny. This is such a big deal that Princeton theologian John Murray commented, 'Union with Christ is the central truth of the whole doctrine of salvation... There is no truth, therefore, more suited to impart confidence and strength, comfort and joy in the Lord than this one of union with Christ' (John Murray, *Redemption: Accomplished and Applied*, pp. 170, 171).

W.W.J.D?: What Would Jesus Do? A question intended to help us follow in the footsteps of Jesus. True sanctification creates true holiness, and true holiness is doing what Jesus would do. This question often has the unintended consequence of sending us forth on a futile endeavor to imitate the inimitable *by human strength alone*. For you to do what Jesus would do requires three factors: 1) salvation and the new identity it brings; 2) the power of Christ through the Holy Spirit; 3) a consistent faith, which is itself the product of consistent spiritual growth and maturity.

Appendix

The Parable of the Prodigal Son

To illustrate the point further, Jesus told them this story: 'A man had two sons. The younger son told his father, "I want my share of your estate now, instead of waiting until you die." So his father agreed to divide his wealth between his sons:

> *A few days later this younger son packed all his belongings and took a trip to a distant land, and there he wasted all his money on wild living. About the time his money ran out, a great famine swept over the land, and he began to starve. He persuaded a local farmer to hire him to feed his pigs. The boy became so hungry that even the pods he was feeding the pigs looked good to him. But no one gave him anything.*

'When he finally came to his senses, he said to himself, "At home even the hired men have food enough to spare, and here I am, dying of hunger! I will go home to my father and say, 'Father, I have sinned against both heaven and you, and I am no longer worthy of being called your son. Please take me on as a hired man.'"

'So he returned home to his father. And while he was still a long distance away, his father saw him coming. Filled with love and compassion, he ran to his son, embraced him, and kissed him. His son said to him, "Father, I have sinned against both heaven and you, and I am no longer worthy of being called your son."

'But his father said to the servants, "Quick! Bring the

finest robe in the house and put it on him. Get a ring for his finger, and sandals for his feet. And kill the calf we have been fattening in the pen. We must celebrate with a feast, for this son of mine was dead and has now returned to life. He was lost, but now he is found." So the party began.

'Meanwhile, the older son was in the fields working. When he returned home, he heard music and dancing in the house, and he asked one of the servants what was going on. "Your brother is back", he was told, "and your father has killed the calf we were fattening and has prepared a great feast. We are celebrating because of his safe return."

'The older brother was angry and wouldn't go in. His father came out and begged him, but he replied, "All these years I've worked hard for you and never once refused to do a single thing you told me to. And in all that time you never gave me even one young goat for a feast with my friends. Yet when this son of yours comes back after squandering your money on prostitutes, you celebrate by killing the finest calf we have."

'His father said to him, "Look, dear son, you and I are very close, and everything I have is yours. We had to celebrate this happy day. For your brother was dead and has come back to life! He was lost, but now he is found!"' (Luke 15:11–32, NLT).

Notes

Chapter One: Your Inner Mess

1. C.S. Lewis. *Mere Christianity*, in *The Complete C.S. Lewis Signature Classics*, New York: HarperCollins, 2008, page 78.

2. C.S. Lewis, edited by Walter Hooper. 'Eden's Courtesy' in *Poems*, San Diego: Harcourt Brace and Company, 1964, page 98.

3. Stephen King, *On Writing*, New York: Pocket Books, 2000, pages 96, 7.

Chapter Two: Your Inner Sinner

1. http://www.barna.org/FlexPage.aspx?Page=BarnaUpdate&BarnaUpdateID=219

2. Colossians 3:12; 1 John 3:17, Proverbs 23:16. Today's translations recognize these bodily references as metaphors for emotional states.

Chapter Three: Your Inner Saint

1. *The Worm Song*. Copyright 1975, Bob Giovannetti. Used by permission.

Chapter Four: Your Inner Jerk

1. https://www.fatherhood.org/father_factor.asp. All the fatherhood data in this chapter is compiled from this website.

2. Snell, Tracy L. and Danielle C. Morton. Women in Prison: Survey of Prison Inmates, 1991. Bureau of Justice Statistics Special Report, Washington, D.C.: U.S. Department of Justice, 1994: 4.

3. Connee Bush, Ronald L. Mullis and Ann K. Mullis. 'Differences in Empathy Between Offender and Nonoffender Youth.' *Journal of Youth and Adolescence* 29 (August 2000), 467–478.

4. Hoffmann, John P. 'The Community Context of Family Structure and Adolescent Drug Use.' *Journal of Marriage and Family* 64 (May 2002), 314–330.

5. Sedlak, Andrea J. and Diane D. Broadhurst. *The Third National Incidence Study of Child Abuse and Neglect: Final Report.* U.S. Department of Health and Human Services. National Center on Child Abuse and Neglect, Washington, D.C., September 1996.

6. Teachman, Jay D. 'The Childhood Living Arrangements of Children and the Characteristics of Their Marriages.' *Journal of Family Issues* 25 (January 2004), 86–111.

Chapter Five: Your Inner Dummy

1. Charles H. Spurgeon. 'Anxiety, Ambition, Indecision' in *The Metropolitan Tabernacle Pulpit*, sermon #2871 at http://www.spurgeon.org/sermons/2871.htm

Chapter Six: Your Inner Brat

1. Names have been changed. http://www.courttv.com/news/scm/scm_030702.html

2. Kokoloski-Young vs. Coca Cola Enterprises, et al., State of Michigan, Court of Appeals, March 28, 2006. Case No. 264119, Wayne Circuit Court.

Chapter Seven: Your Inner Thug

1. Sticklers for detail will note that some boxing authorities considered Terrell the champion and Ali the challenger.

2. www.usatoday.com/sports/century/alifs11

Chapter Eight: Your C.I.A. Agent

1. C.S. Lewis. *The Four Loves*, San Diego: Harcourt, Inc., 1988, page 121.

Chapter Nine: Grace

1. John Ortberg, *Everybody's Normal Till You Get to Know Them*, Grand Rapids, MI: Zondervan, 2003.

Chapter Ten: The Cross

1. Hal Lindsey, *Satan Is Alive and Well on Planet Earth*, Grand Rapids, MI: Zondervan, 1972. The last few chapters were later republished under a different title: *The Guilt Trip*, Uhrichsville, OH: Barbour Publishing, 1996.

2. Micah 7:19; Isaiah 38:17; Hebrews 10:17; Isaiah 1:18.

3. You can read the instructions in Leviticus 16:5–14.

4. Adapted from Erwin Lutzer, *Cries from the Cross: A Journey into the Heart of Jesus*, Chicago, IL: Moody Publishers, 2002.

5. 1972 *New Testament in Modern English* by J. B. Phillips.

Chapter Eleven: The Galvanized Life

1. Quoted in Augustus H. Strong, *Systematic Theology*, Philadelphia, PA: The Griffith and Rowland Press, 1909, page 808.

2. See Romans 7:1–6.

3. A. B. Simpson, *The Fourfold Gospel*, pages 31, 32, public domain.

Chapter Twelve: Faith

1. Eugene Peterson, *A Long Obedience in the Same Direction*, San Marcos, CA: Hovel Audio.

Chapter Thirteen: Community

1. Herbert W. Lockyer, *All the Apostles of the Bible*, Grand Rapids, MI: Zondervan, 1988.

2. Peter Lewis, 'Do You Want To Play?' in *Fast Company* [November 2007], page 113.

3. See the heartwarming details at: http://www.corrieweb.nl/amazon/historicax14.htm and at: http://en.wikipedia.org/wiki/List_of_famous_duels

4. Ebenezer Cobham Brewer, *The Reader's Handbook of Allusions, References, Plots, and Stories*, Philadelphia: J.B. Lippincott Co., 1889, page 231, public domain.

5. Gipsy Smith, an Irish evangelist, quoted in Ravi Zacharias and Norman Geisler, eds, *Is Your Church Ready? Motivating Leaders to Live an Apologetic Life*, Zondervan, 2003, page 22.

Chapter Fourteen: The Grace Drill

1. Ray C. Stedman, *Reason to Rejoice: Love, Grace and Forgiveness in Paul's Letter to the Romans*, Grand Rapids, MI: Discovery House Publishers, 2004. Online at: www.raystedman. org/romans2/romans3

Chapter Fifteen: Two Scripts

1. Francis Schaeffer, *True Spirituality*, Wheaton, IL: Tyndale House, 1975, page 59.

2. The word for stern (*prumne*) can refer either to the rear of the boat or to an inside cabin. Since the boat was filling with water, it is safe to assume he was at the rear, perhaps under a canopy.

3. Cf. 2 Timothy 1:7. Liddell–Scott–Jones Lexicon of Classical Greek, in the passage already cited.

4. Scripture taken from The Holy Bible, 21st Century King James Version (KJ21), Copyright 1994, Deuel Enterprises, Inc., Gary, SD 57237, and used by permission.

5. I first learned these lines at a life-transforming men's retreat led by Jim Dethmer and Bob Sloan.

6. A.B. Simpson, *Wholly Sanctified*, public domain, chapter one. www.gospeljohn.com/ simpson_whollysanctified1

Chapter Sixteen: The Secret Weapon

1. Henry Drummond, *The Greatest Thing in the World* (1874), public domain.

2. William Oncken, Jr. and Donald L. Wass. 'Management time: Who's got the monkey?' in *Harvard Business Review* Volume 52, Number 6, November–December, 1974, 75–80.

3. 'The vast majority of criminals are normal people driven by the same motives that drive us all... both criminal and non-criminal behavior are expressions of the same needs and values.' Ezzat A. Fattah, 'The Rational Choice/Opportunity Perspectives as a Vehicle for Integrating Criminological and Victimological Theories,' in Ronald V. Clarke and Marcus Felson, *Routine Activity and Rational Choice*, Piscataway, NJ: Transaction Publishers, 1993, page 229.

4. Oswald Chambers, *My Utmost for His Highest*. Devotional dated September 17.

Recommended Readings

These books offer various biblical perspectives on dealing with your flesh/Inner Mess and on living a whole, holy lifestyle. Some are classics, others are new. Most of them are meaty; I hope they give you a better grasp of Christ's power to corral your Inner Mess.

Barber, Wayne A. *Living Grace: Letting Jesus Be Jesus In You*. Nashville: B&H Publishing Group, 2005.

Baxter, J. Sidlow. *His Deeper Work in Us: An Inquiry into New Testament Teaching on the Subject of Christian Holiness*. Grand Rapids: Zondervan, 1974.

Bridges, Jerry. *The Discipline of Grace: God's Role and Our Role in the Pursuit of Holiness*. Colorado Springs: NavPress, 1994.

Bridges, Jerry. *The Pursuit of Holiness*. Colorado Springs: NavPress, 2006.

Chambers, Oswald. *My Utmost For His Highest*. Barbour Publishing, 2000.

Evans, Tony. *Free At Last: Experiencing Your True Freedom Through Your Identity in Christ*. Eugene, OR: Harvest House, 2005.

Gillham, William and Preston H. *Lifetime Guarantee*. Eugene, OR: Harvest House, 1993.

Kendall, R.T. *How to Forgive Ourselves Totally: Begin Again by Breaking Free from Past Mistakes*. Lake Mary, FL: Charisma House, 2007.

Ironside, H. A. *Holiness: the False and the True*. New York: Loizeaux Brothers, 1912.

Lundgaard, Kris. *The Enemy Within: Straight Talk about the Power and Defeat of Sin*. Phillipsburg, NJ: P & R Publishing, 1998.

Lutzer, Erwin W. *After You've Blown It: Reconnecting with God and Others*. Portland: Multnomah, 2004.

Lutzer, Erwin W. *Winning the Inner War: How to Say No to a Stubborn Habit*. Wheaton: Victor Books, 2002.

Mahaney, C.J. *Living the Cross-Centered Life*. Portland: Multnomah, 2006.

McGrath, Alister E. *The Journey*. New York: Doubleday, 1999.

Meyer, F. B. *Fit for the Master's Use*. Costa Mesa: Calvary Chapel Books, 2002.

Meyer, F. B. *Abide in Christ*. New Kensington, PA: Whitaker House Publishers, n.d.

Murray, Andrew. *The Secret of Spiritual Strength*. New Kensington, PA: Whittaker House Publishers, 1997.

Nee, Watchman. *Sit, Walk, Stand*. Wheaton: Tyndale House, 1977.

Nee, Watchman. *The Normal Christian Life*. Wheaton: Tyndale House, 2007.

Packer, J.I. *Knowing God: Twentieth Anniversary Edition*. Downers Grove, IL: Inter-varsity Press, 1993.

Peterson, Eugene. *A Long Obedience in the Same Direction: Twentieth Anniversary Edition*. Downers Grove, IL: Inter-varsity Press, 2000.

Pink, Arthur W. *Life of Faith: What Has God Done For You?* Fearn, Scotland: Christian Focus Publications, (reprint) 1998.

Ryle, J.C. *Holiness: Its Nature, Hindrances, Difficulties, and Roots*. Peabody, MA: Hendrickson Publishers, 2007.

Schaeffer, Francis. *True Spirituality*. Wheaton: Tyndale House, 1972.

Simpson, A. B. *Christ in You: The Christ-Life and the Self-Life*. Camp Hill: Christian Publications Inc, 1977.

Smalley, Gary. *Change Your Heart, Change Your Life*. Nashville: Thomas Nelson, 2007.

Spurgeon, Charles H. *A Passion for Holiness in A Believer's Life*. Greenville: Emerald Books, 1966.

Taylor, Howard, *Dr and Mrs Hudson Taylor's Spiritual Secret*. London: China Inland Mission, 1935.

Thomas, W. H. Griffith. *Christianity is Christ*. London: Longmans, Green and Co., 1916.

Thomas, Major W. Ian. *The Saving Life of Christ*. Grand Rapids: Zondervan, 1988.

Tozer, A.W. *The Knowledge of the Holy*. San Francisco: Harper, 1978.

Tozer, A.W. *Man: The Dwelling Place of God*. Harrisburg: Christian Publications, Inc., 1966.

Trumbull, Charles. *Victory in Christ*. Portland: Multnomah, (reprint) 2004.

Wilkinson, Bruce. *Secrets of the Vine*. Portland: Multnomah, 2006.